D0016798

BETHEL SEMINARY WEST
LIBRARY
4747 College Avenue
San Diego, California 92115

# SERMON SEEDS FROM THE GOSPELS

251
G242

# SERMON SEEDS FROM
# The Gospels

## BY WEBB B. GARRISON

FLEMING H. REVELL COMPANY

COPYRIGHT © MCMLVIII, BY FLEMING H. REVELL COMPANY

*Printed in the United States of America*

Library of Congress Catalog Card Number: 58-11018


Westwood, New Jersey
London E.C.4—29 Ludgate Hill
Glasgow C.2—229 Bothwell Street

*To*
*Mabel Rebecca*

# CONTENTS

# PREFACE

That complex process whose mystery we hide under the label, "getting an idea," can be controlled only partially. New understanding may be said to "come" just as truly as it may be described as being "found." Neither the time nor the place of insight can be predicted.

Frenzied searching on Saturday night may be fruitless, forcing a choice between no sermon next day and taken-for-granted exposition of a hackneyed idea. Yet at a wholly unexpected moment, in the midst of activities not focused upon sermonizing, one may stumble upon a dynamic new interpretation—or be seized and taken captive by it.

The notes in this volume were made over a period of about ten years. They were jotted down under all kinds of conditions: while riding trains and planes, snatching a ten-minute devotional at the barber shop, turning to St. John for a Scripture break instead of a coffee break, and exploring the fresh language of unfamiliar translations.

Only one element characterizes all the seeds in this packet—each is a capsule exposition of an idea that is fresh in the thought of the compiler. Socially, it may be very old; to this individual reader of the Gospels, it is new. It is a grain of truth discovered in viewing the New Testament story through the lens of one personality.

Because this material is so personal, it is not likely that any user will be struck by more than a fraction of the ideas suggested.

Nor are any of them expanded to the extent of a suggested outline. Springboards for thought are offered here—points of departure rather than maps and timetables.

Hence the maximum harvest can be gained from these little seeds by cultivating some of them in the rich soil of one's own life and thought. Temporarily discarding those paragraphs that do not strike fire, skim through until half a dozen more or less provocative ones are found. Then mull over them until they begin to tease at the mind in such fashion that fresh insights emerge —perhaps radically different from the interpretations that served as starting points of thought.

So treated, this little volume becomes a kit of tools rather than a finished product. May you use its contents to build many an intellectual and spiritual edifice that is uniquely your own.

WEBB B. GARRISON

# SERMON SEEDS FROM THE GOSPELS

# THE GOSPEL OF
# Matthew

*. . . the son of David, the son of Abraham (Matthew 1:1).*

Much has been made of the inconsistency and blindness of gospel writers who tell the story of birth from a virgin—but include the family tree of the father. This is often used to discredit the story.

Such a view is a complete distortion, a failure to look through eyes of the evangelist. We must not suppose that Matthew was naïve. He knew the facts of life. But knowing them, he gave Joseph's family tree—not to dilute the element of the incredible, but to magnify it. Instead of trying to explain away a difficulty, he blithely underscored it. His purpose was not to reduce the story of the marvelous Babe to mild improbability but to exalt it to complete and glorious incredibility.

Many persons have gagged over the doctrine that Jesus was the child of the Holy Spirit. But these same analysts have usually taken it as a commonplace fact that he was a descendant of David and Abraham. It is easy to overlook the marvels and mysteries of human heredity—the altogether astonishing fact that there is continuity in the stream of life. Compared with the wonders of biology, the mysteries of Christian dogma are almost simple.

*. . . and David the king begat Solomon of her that had been the wife of Urias (Matthew 1:6).*

What a strange turn of events! The wife of Urias, Bathsheba, is a link in the chain leading to birth of the Saviour! In the case of a chain, there are no nonessential parts. Each is 100 per cent important. Man is too limited to appraise the full meaning of any event or process, contemporary or historical. That which lies in the past must be continually re-appraised. That which occurs in the present is darkly obscure. That which lies in the future is so wholly beyond control or prediction, whether for triumph or for woe, that all pronouncements about it, doleful or jolly, are limited in their validity. History is plastic, unfinished, and beyond complete analysis.

*But while he thought on these things, behold, the angel of the Lord appeared unto him . . . (Matthew 1:20).*

Joseph was actively seeking the solution to a difficult problem. He prepared his mind for revelation by stretching his own capacities and arriving at a state of receptivity—even expectancy. His mental soil was well prepared for a seed to fall upon it and sprout. So his vision was far from casual or accidental.

Angels are most likely to appear when God-seekers are profoundly troubled, looking for divine meaning in a problem situation and positive that such meaning can be found, hence eagerly striving to attain it. To be sure that some variety of divine messenger will bring an answer, and to struggle with a life-shaking problem, are the two chief human conditions to be met in order to be visited by angels.

*. . . behold, there came wise men from the east to Jerusalem (Matthew 2:1).*

Two groups of men, and only two, are named by the gospel

writers as being aware of the strange and marvelous things taking place in Bethlehem.

It was not accidental that shepherds and magi took notice of God's break-through into history; both were outside the stream of pious, orthodox Judaism. Wise men saw the star and its meaning from a great distance: in geography and ideas. Religious leaders in Jerusalem were much closer in both space and ideas—but were not stimulated to see. Always, the advantages gained by proximity and expertness are accompanied by liabilities. So the veteran and the expert should listen with eager interest when an amateur or stranger earnestly advocates a novel idea.

*When Herod the king had heard these things, he was troubled . . . (Matthew 2:3).*

Afraid of a baby! What a delightfully mad paradox!

Such fear seems strange at first look but is pervasive and prevailing. It still exists. Every dictator and demagogue is afraid— desperately afraid. He fears that babies will grow up and challenge him. No matter what his power, he knows that a helpless infant is a bundle of possibilities, with potential capacity to overthrow empires.

*. . . bring me word again, that I may come and worship him also (Matthew 2:8).*

Many weighty problems are raised by this command. Was Herod entirely and hopelessly hypocritical at this time? Did he use this explanation as fancy dress to hide his own plan to murder —or was he at the moment really receptive to new ideas?

Who dares to pronounce the final word on this subject?

To a degree, each of us is like Herod. We tell the world that we want to find the highest truth in such controversial areas as race relations and peace. Yet all the while we seek that truth our loyalties are in chaos. There is always danger that a quest launched in good faith may end in a cry for blood.

15

*When they saw the star, they rejoiced with exceeding great joy (Matthew 2:10).*

To find a guide when lost, a sure point of reference in a state of bewilderment, is indeed a cause for great joy. Men cannot live effectively without such guides—fixed centers around which to organize the journey of life. The church has the privilege and solemn obligation of lifting up stars to catch the eyes of eager but somewhat befuddled men, motivated by idealism and close to the Christ Child, but not quite sure which way to go in order actually to find Him.

*. . . they presented unto him gifts; gold, and frankincense, and myrrh (Matthew 2:11).*

Here is a fresh Christmas sermon . . . .

What strange gifts to bestow on a baby! But wait . . . These men were neither naïve nor impulsive. They had engaged in long planning and were very wise. Yet they brought the Babe things not understandable nor immediately usable by Him.

Many of the finest things that can be given a child are quite beyond his comprehension so long as he remains in infancy—and will not be purposefully used by him for years. Such gifts are values, ideals, habits, and all that we call "education." We spend considerable time selecting Christmas gifts such as toys; sometimes we neglect to deliberate equally long about gifts of attitudes and habits.

*. . . they departed into their own country another way (Matthew 2:12).*

There is no way one can spend his or her entire life kneeling in the straw beside the manger, offering precious gifts to the Holy Child. We must inevitably go back to our own country, lose immediate physical contact with the highest and best found in a life of searching.

Does this lead to despair, to resignation, to ceasing from beginning to search?

By no means. For the one central event, self-giving in the stable, becomes the organizing center for all future activity. Through memory, it can transform life in spite of the fact that one cannot continue endlessly in the physical presence of glory.

Men can no more be always at their prayers than they can be always eating or sleeping. We must come down from every mountaintop. But we do not need to come down the same persons we were when we ascended.

*Arise, . . . and flee into Egypt, and be thou there until I bring thee word . . . (Matthew 2:13).*

Joseph and Mary, with the Babe, went far away into a strange country—and there listened for a message from an angel.

To go along life's highway—or any segment of it—listening for angels! That immediately and automatically gives direction and tone to the journey. It reduces the tendency to be impatient and querulous. It makes one rise with eager hope every morning: "Perhaps this is the day!" It encourages tolerance of bad travelling conditions. It lessens one's readiness to be guided by reports of other travellers whose goals and motives are different.

*. . . Out of Egypt have I called my son (Matthew 2:15).*

Egypt symbolizes both captivity and idolatry. In the first century, it was regarded as the international den of iniquity. Yet God used Egypt in the drama of salvation! There may be special roles that all the world's Egypts can play—provided we are willing to listen when angels tell us how to act in regard to them.

No Egypt is hopeless, to be scorned and abandoned. At any moment, any Egypt may include a child of God who will come out to be a leader of men. Part of the tragedy of man is his capacity to develop Egypts; much of his glory comes to focus in the fact that none is a closed door. From the most unlikely neighborhood, and even from a family that offers special promise by few human standards, may come a bringer of light. Even in Egypt, a child is a bundle of potentialities too big for the wisest to measure.

*But when he saw many of the Pharisees and Sadducees come to his baptism, he said unto them, O generation of vipers, who hath warned you to flee from the wrath to come? (Matthew 3:7).*

John's harsh words sound almost out of character in the mouth of an evangelist, however stern. They suggest at least two warnings. Church groups should not be so eager to *count* converts that they ignore personal qualities of those whom they include in their statistical reports. And the words of John also imply that some attempts to flee from divine wrath are based upon strictly selfish motives; that is, the power of the ego is so tremendous that even an act of dedication can be motivated by self-interest.

These matters underscore man's predicament: we cannot save ourselves, for we can never entirely overcome ourselves. Something must be done for us as well as by us. John evidently felt that these men had not yet assumed the attitude of surrender that is essential to divine rescue symbolized by baptism. They wished to participate in rites that—for them—were empty and meaningless. Though eager to be delivered from the coming wrath and willing to be baptized by the prophet, they trusted in their good works rather than in the miraculous delivery of God.

*. . . lo, the heavens were opened unto him, and he saw the Spirit of God descending like a dove, and lighting upon him (Matthew 3:16).*

This profound encounter with God the Father was an accompaniment of participation in human ceremonial conducted by a man who felt and expressed his unworthiness (verse 14). Ritual is a major channel of grace; it is helpful even though it may not be essential and may appear perfunctory or inappropriate. For ceremonial is not simply something to be performed for its own sake. It is not a terminus, but a road. It is a way toward encounter

18

with God. Ritual may serve to focus the attention at the same time that it arouses the emotions and constrains eyes, ears, nose, and other bodily senses in order to concentrate the whole self upon a single goal. Purposefully followed, it is powerful.

*Then was Jesus led up of the Spirit . . . to be tempted . . . (Matthew 4:1).*

That the Spirit was the leader here comes as a disturbing thought, at first. But God can and does have a part in temptation. Had God not created a world in which temptation is included, there could have been no context in which to achieve real manhood. Temptation can be a means of growth. Indeed, it is always a means toward either growth or recession; that is, temptation is never static, but always divisive—an either/or force in life.

*And when he had fasted forty days and forty nights, he was afterward an hungred (Matthew 4:2).*

During a period of passionate seeking, spiritual exercises are likely so to absorb the attention that Satan may hammer on the door without being noticed. But inevitably there comes the moment when relaxed attention leads to the startling realization that one is hungry.

It is possible to focus on the spirit only so long; then the long-ignored body clamors for attention. This resurgence of material concerns after deep devotional striving is inevitable, and hence no cause for despair. It is the moment Satan always seizes to press his claims. Awareness that he will come does not keep him away, but may help in resistance to him.

This soul-body and spiritual-material dualism is such that man can never long escape struggle, whether it be called temptation or not. No matter how hard one may try, he cannot remain on an even keel in any outlook or practice or motive. There are cycles of movement in every field of endeavor and each relationship. High moments are as certain to be followed by lower ones as night is to follow day. Though peaks of the mountains may be continually raised and depth of the valleys diminished during life, the reality of up-and-down waverings is inescapable. See, for example, William Cowper's hymn, "Oh for a Closer Walk with God." This is the testimony of every great mystic and saint.

Since the experience is universal, "hunger" in the spiritual or intellectual or moral or physical sense is not to be condemned and denounced. Rather, it is to be accepted and utilized as a stimulus for seeking higher, nobler experiences in the future. It is a point of rebound, a foundation for a new upward leap. In this sense, despair can be the most stimulating and enriching of all experiences short of the mystical rapture itself. Without despair the ecstatic sense of spiritual victory would certainly come to no person more than once during life, if at all.

*. . . Man shall not live by bread alone, but by every word that proceedeth out of the mouth of God (Matthew 4:4).*

A sensitive man, seeing evidence of hunger and need, may be so challenged that he gives his whole attention to the attempt to feed the hungry and alleviate physical suffering. This is not only a first, but also a most subtle temptation, for it presumes that food is more important than ideas. Jesus' warning does not minimize social service, but underscores the fact that even feeding the hungry must be a means to a higher end rather than a goal in itself.

*. . . Thou shalt not tempt the Lord thy God (Matthew 4:7).*

Every test that any man can use is man-made, and hence limited. It partakes of the creaturehood of the tester. So it cannot test or measure God—who is above all man's categories and measurements.

Being inherently incapable of testing God, the person who tries to do so can never succeed in doing anything more than test himself. This is self-judgment with a vengeance.

Man must accept his creaturehood, his inability to measure or to challenge God. Arriving at this point of view, one ceases to fret over what he does not understand. He accepts mysteries cheerfully, and is not bothered by what, according to human standards, seem to be inconsistencies in the divine character.

*And they immediately left the ship and their father, and followed him (Matthew 4:22).*

Even allowing for telescoping of the time element in telling the story, quick and radical action is indicated here.

Perhaps a certain recklessness is an asset in the search for God. Those who are too reluctant to take a chance, too wedded to old, known, safe, comfortable ways, are not willing to engage in the adventure of adopting a new idea or following another master.

One can be too reckless, can run to adopt every new fashion in thought and to support each fresh aspirant for leadership. But within institutional religion, the number who err in this fashion is trifling in comparison with those who insist on staying with dad and the ship.

*. . . I am not come to destroy, but to fulfil (Matthew 5:17).*

Enlargement and completion are quite different processes from destruction. Yet they are like it in involving change—which may be disturbing and difficult to accept. There can be no self-realization of a seed, for example, without "destruction" as a way to enlargement. We must not resist that change which, though painful, leads to fulfilment.

*. . . whosoever shall say, Thou fool, shall be in danger of hell fire (Matthew 5:22).*

This last in the trinity of offenses is the most fearful. It is also the most obscure. Offenses which men take seriously and about which they legislate may actually be less vital than underlying attitudes from which crimes spring.

Pride is involved here. This is the deepest of sins and the most versatile in assuming disguises. Because it is alien to the humble and the seeking, possession of it is a sign of one's lost state.

Any man proud enough to condemn his brother (by comparison with himself) is too proud to be really humble before God. In passing judgment, he assumes a function of the Father. He plays at being Judge of the world, and of men. This brings his attention to focus on the shortcomings of other men, rather than upon his own failures. Comparing others with himself, he labels them fools and by implication makes himself seem wise. Feeling that he has achieved, he has really lost. Considering himself to be good, he has actually become evil. He is a rebel under sentence of condemnation—but doesn't recognize his own state.

*Leave . . . be reconciled to thy brother, and then come and offer thy gift (Matthew 5:24).*

Entering the place of the altar in holy fear, one may hear the voice of God in a special way. That voice serves as an awakener, reminding of specific things the seeker may do to make himself more suitable to talk with God. Kneeling in the holy place, he gains new perspective, sees with new eyes for the moment.

So the admonition that insights and revelations of the altar should bear fruit in action is a valid one. It is not set up as a barrier to keep men from the place of dedication. Rather, it is a powerful incentive that they should come—in order to gain the transformations that can result.

*Neither shalt thou swear by thy head, because thou canst not make one hair white or black (Matthew 5:36).*

Here is vivid testimony to the limitedness of man! In an age of rinses and bleaches, all our changes are temporary and restricted. We do not have power to change the color of a single hair—but can modify just a part of its external structure. We manipulate trifles with skill, but cannot touch basic things.

*And if ye salute your brethren only, what do ye more than others?*
*. . . (Matthew 5:47).*

We do not have to agree on details of the faith and "come from
the same household" in order to treat one another with respect
and courtesy. Men who are vigorous in preaching world peace can
sometimes find neighbors in enemy uniforms—but overlook them
in their own neighborhood. This is more than a call to ordinary
tolerance of the individual who wears a label: Catholic, Jew,
Amish. This is a challenge to look for common values and goals
held by members of groups that are divided from one another.

*Take heed that ye do not your alms before men, to be seen of
them . . . (Matthew 6:1).*

It is a terrific temptation to perform socially approved acts for
the sake of group commendation—that is, to be guided by human
and cultural norms as well as to seek satisfaction of selfish motives.
This is the chief indictment against "How to Win Friends and
Influence People." Part of the damnable feature of the business
is that it actually *works* in a rather significant fashion. Men who
seek to impress others are likely to succeed, though not always in
a degree sufficient to satisfy their own wants. But the process
of winning success in this fashion inhibits a course of action that
can lead to winning the rewards of heaven.

So the warning of Jesus involves not so much the operation of
justice as of cause and effect. It is a basic law of God, at once
hidden and clear, that "you get what you pay for."

Be careful, then, what goals you select: you are not only likely
to reach them but arrival at one precludes the simultaneous
winning of another. There is an element of finality and exclusive-
ness here.

*. . . Take no thought . . . for your body, what ye shall put on . . .
(Matthew 6:25).*

Concern over clothing is one special and vivid aspect of slavery to material values. Though more easily condemned and more obvious than some other types of materialism, it is neither better nor worse than they.

Extravagant display such as that which culminates in wearing costly clothing and heavy jewelry is the obvious butt of the argument here. But not so readily apparent is the fact that one can be concerned about putting on garments that say to others: "See how devout and unselfish this man is!" It is possible to practice studied neglect and boastful poverty, as well (though not so frequently) as purposeful extravagance. Thus, the wearing of a religious garb—or restricting one's self to a flimsy suit and one pair of old shoes—can become a goal instead of a way of dedication.

Thing-linked wants and values pursue men so relentlessly that there is no monastery into which one may flee for automatic haven. To deceive ourselves into thinking that we can fully achieve the standard of "slavery to God" is the greatest impiety and blindness of all. Analyze any command in the group to which this belongs, and the one conclusion that is valid for every man is confession: "I am a sinner. God help me and redeem me from paying the price of my sin."

*Consider the lilies of the field, how they grow . . . (Matthew 6:28).*

This is another of Jesus' impossible challenges. For no man can wholly tear away the veil that hides secrets of how the lilies grow. We can marvel at the beauty of their blossoms and enjoy their fragrance without pretending to comprehend their metabolism and interaction with the total environment.

For practical purposes, meaning of the lily's growth is that it takes place through God's providence and plan, without conscious (logical and reasoned) labor. That is, the flower, necessarily, thrusts itself upon God. It can do nothing else.

In some respects, such dependence is passive. Though true to the forces that guide its development and its total life form, there is no planning or worry here. Any man who can achieve a state approaching such basic trust in God's providence is thereby equipped to become a poet or a painter—or a saint.

*Take therefore no thought for the morrow . . . (Matthew 6:34).*
This prescription for a free, happy, worry-less life is not to be taken in isolation. It is valid only within a special context. Without the "therefore," the injunction is easily distorted; for it rests on the broad views laid down above, verses 24-33, and strikes at that "slavery to material things" which prevents one from becoming a slave to God.

Here, then, is a special instance of the general principle that no man can serve two masters. That person who sits about fretting over food and clothing tomorrow or next year or in old age, by the very process of directing attention to these material goals, inhibits and restricts the possibility of bringing attention to focus upon search for the Kingdom.

Much of modern life is predicated upon the proposition that we must be continually anxious about tomorrow. Insurance and social security are programs designed to help one to "take thought about the morrow." Pushed to their extreme positions, such programs say that tomorrow is in some fashion more important than today —we must give up some of the things wanted and perhaps needed now, because it is possible (though by no means certain) that later, we shall be in greater need than at present.

That state of mind to which the text points is not the vacuum of laziness or resignation. Rather, it is the positive trust of a dynamic faith which rests upon particular values and convictions. By placing one's primary emphasis upon seeking God's Kingdom —in all the complexities that this concept involves—one has neither time nor energy nor enthusiasm to sit about brooding over the future. He is so busy with important things that he cannot give attention to the trivial matter of whether or not he shall eat tomorrow.

25

*Sufficient unto the day is the evil thereof (Matthew 6:34).*

Such is the nature of life that no day—not one—can escape the impact of evil. If one wrestles positively with the evil of each day, he will be too busy to stew over that anticipated in the future. What a strange preventive of worry!

*And why beholdest thou the mote that is in thy brother's eye, but considerest not the beam that is in thine own eye? (Matthew 7:3).*

This teaching is cast in the form of a question. It doesn't ask each individual listener or reader to consider *whether* beams are being overlooked—but *why.* Such a state is universal; no man escapes from it for very long at a time.

Traditional exposition of this question often misses the heart of the matter, assumes that Jesus exhorts His followers to stop overlooking beams and emphasizing motes. Such is far from the case; the Master is actually insisting that seldom is one capable of achieving a state in which he continually pays more heed to his own beams than to his neighbor's motes.

This is no plea for mere tolerance. Rather, it is an urgent challenge to recognize the absolute limitedness and lostness of every individual—who can ponder why he engages in selective viewing without being able fully to eliminate it from his own life.

*Ask, and it shall be given you; seek, and ye shall find; knock, and it shall be opened unto you (Matthew 7:7).*

This is not a promise of material success as a reward for persistence. Emphasis is not upon finding precisely what one seeks, but on the certainty that the ardent seeker will discover *something,* perhaps wholly unexpected, that will more than justify the search.

For the whole passage is oriented toward the seeking of a single goal: membership in the Kingdom, encounter with God, personal discovery of God's power. With this as the great and primary goal, all material hopes are secondary and derived.

Given such a philosophy oriented toward one clear and unshakable goal, the possibility of defeat or failure does not exist. All strivings, including those that bring disappointments on the lower level, will serve to open doors. Sometimes that which is found by accident or in a kind of failure will prove better than anything the seeker had in mind. For we are children to whom the Father must sometimes say "No" in order to speak a larger "Yes" (see verse 11).

*And when Jesus was entered into Capernaum, there came unto him a centurion . . . (Matthew 8:5).*

It is suggestive to take a brief look at the range of persons through whom or in whom Jesus worked miracles. He crossed national boundaries by listening to the plea of the centurion—who was a member of an enemy force, serving in the army of occupation. Jesus healed women, and so crossed the boundary line of sex. He healed children, ignoring intellectual levels. He broke through social barriers by working miracles upon beggars. Even that most difficult of walls—intimacy—was broken in the working of a miracle upon Peter's mother-in-law: a member of the intimate circle.

Such a list, which is far from exhaustive, suggests that wherever there is a person, there is potential for miracle. No barrier is final. No member of any group is wholly excluded. Divine encounter may break through any barricade whatever in order to release creative power in the most improbable times and places.

*. . . and she arose, and ministered unto them (Matthew 8:15).*

Healed of her fever, the mother of Peter's wife might have reacted in one of many ways: exuberant joy, incredulity, desire to run tell the neighbors, or even near-indifference. Matthew doesn't tell us how she felt about the miracle, but he does indicate what she did: she went about the ordinary chores of a hostess.

After a cure, it is well to get a job and go to work. One who has been healed by any method can help bring the healing to mature fruition by serving God and society in a definite task.

*. . . Then he arose, and rebuked the winds and the sea; and there was a great calm (Matthew 8:26).*

Power to manipulate physical processes and effects never fails to evoke admiration. We still marvel at anyone who finds a fresh way to master winds and tides and waves.

Yet the basic message here is not in the physical miracle. It has to do with the wonderful and unbelievable fact that Jesus has power to lead all men into a calm way of life—such that the storms about us bring no fears. Actually to quiet the fears of a person is a feat comparable to the taming of an ocean. But because it is less tangible, we do not so easily observe its impact and seldom regard it so highly.

*. . . Jesus seeing their faith said unto the sick of the palsy; Son, be of good cheer; thy sins be forgiven thee (Matthew 9:2).*

Persons of His day considered Jesus to be a religious heretic. Many of our day regard His statement as medical heresy.

Part of our human dilemma lies in our respect for boundaries. They are essential for thought and action but are conventional and arbitrary. Great innovations nearly always stem from shutting one's eyes to some set of accepted boundaries. This has been demonstrated many times in scientific discovery. It also applies to such problems as race relations, where the crux of the matter is the definition of "race." Just as Jesus paid no attention to the conventional boundary that placed the question of physical health apart from that of spiritual health, so one may succeed in disregarding such boundaries as "Jew," "Catholic," and "Russian."

*. . . he saw a man, named Matthew, sitting at the receipt of custom: and he saith unto him, Follow me (Matthew 9:9).*

Obedience must precede understanding as well as stem from it. There is no simple one-way flow. Rather, there are feed-back effects in both directions. Matthew went straight from the toll office into the band of intimate disciples, with no hint of instruction or delay for participation in a membership class. If one waits to gain complete mastery of Christian thought before beginning to follow Jesus, he will never take the first step.

*. . . They that be whole need not a physician, but they that are sick (Matthew 9:12).*

Here is an echo of the emphasis presented quite differently in 7:3. For the statement is ironic. No man is well; all are sick. But it is only the "sinners"—as opposed to the consciously-righteous Pharisees—who can recognize their own need of medicine. Only an admittedly sick man will open his door to the knock of a physician, however eminent and well qualified he may be to treat the illness involved.

*. . . Jesus came into the ruler's house, and saw the minstrels and the people making a noise (Matthew 9:23).*

Noisy music and pageantry of ceremonial grief may serve to hide from participants the fact that they are dull and blind, incapable of distinguishing between death and sleep. Mourning can be a cloak for spiritual anemia, a camouflage for the fact that the mourner holds material values to be final.

*But go rather to the lost sheep of the house of Israel (Matthew 10:6).*

Of all unlikely places, Israel herself was a haven for lost sheep! She who prided herself on being the guardian of revelation was largely made up of men lurching about blindly!

Perhaps the most bewildered persons in any culture are those who by descent and nominal loyalty belong "within the fold" and hence devote their energies largely to the task of looking condescendingly at Gentiles and Samaritans outside.

*Provide neither gold, nor silver, nor brass in your purses (Matthew 10:9).*

A material reserve provides an avenue of escape, a way of turning back from the primary goal when the going becomes rough.

Reliance on it is a way of disguising the old demon of material values in order to make it acceptable; money in one's wallet or on deposit in the bank promises that there's always something to fall back upon.

Jesus' warning is extreme—almost fanatical. Obedience to His command will reduce the witness to a state of total dependence. He has no reserve, no alternate plan to adopt in the event of failure. The urgency with which the man of empty pockets attacks his commission is a factor adding to the likelihood of his success.

*And if the house be worthy, let your peace come upon it: but if it be not worthy, let your peace return to you (Matthew 10:13).*

Moderns tend to measure the typical service of worship by the zeal and effectiveness of the preacher. There is a general attitude, seldom clearly defined but none the less real, to the effect that "It is up to the man in the pulpit to see that I get something here today."

But that is an absurdity. It ignores the vital and active role of the listener or follower in processes of communication and action. There is no way to provide automatic benefits in religion. Even the blessing of an apostle is conditioned by attitudes and ideas of the recipients. In order to receive abundantly, a listener or follower must work as hard as his leader.

*But the very hairs of your head are all numbered (Matthew 10:30).*

Nothing in the created universe can exist or occur outside the plan of the Creator. Creation is not autonomous. No part of it is subject to caprice or chance. Every aspect of the great, complex whole is related to every other part; there is nothing in isolation. God made and governs the whole integrated system. To think that any part of it may be outside His ken is both folly and treason. Try as he may, man can never escape the burden and opportunity of participating in a God-directed pattern.

30

*He that receiveth a prophet in the name of a prophet shall receive a prophet's reward . . . (Matthew 10:41).*

It is no small task to recognize a prophet. Two men view the same messenger; one sees a spokesman for God, while the other sees a messenger of Satan. We are measured by the list of persons whom we revere. Only one who has the value-system of a prophet will recognize a prophet upon meeting him. See 12:24, 33-35.

*Now when John had heard in the prison the works of Christ, he sent two of his disciples, And said unto him, Art thou he that should come, or do we look for another? (Matthew 11:2-3).*

Imprisoned, John might have become absorbed in nursing a sense of injured innocence. Or he might have devoted all his attention to plans of escape. Instead, the prophet continued to search for answers to basic questions. He did not lose sight of his mission and quest in concern for comfort and safety.

This is an insidious and pervasive problem confronting every seeker. In time of trouble or illness, one may become so absorbed in solving his own problems that he ceases to look for God's anointed.

*And if ye will receive it, this is Elias . . . (Matthew 11:14).*

Ideas are like callers; the householder himself must decide which will be admitted and made comfortable and which will be turned back at the door. To receive an idea is to make room for it in one's system of thought. There is no method by which a messenger of God can transport an idea into the mind of a person who cannot or will not find a place for it.

*. . . thou hast hid these things from the wise and prudent, and hast revealed them unto babes (Matthew 11:25).*

Worldly wisdom constitutes a source of danger, for it is likely to produce pride. To the degree that one is sure he is wise and possesses truth, he is limited in his capacity to receive new thoughts.

31

Hunger must be felt before one is willing to accept food. Though the belly is full of chaff, having no calories, one may still be too full to eat. In order to become empty enough to receive nourishing food, it may be necessary to vomit out the chaff—in the painful and life-transforming process that we call "conversion."

*But I say unto you, That in this place is one greater than the temple (Matthew 12:6).*

Men fashion institutions to conserve and transmit discoveries of individuals. This is an essential process; without institutions of many types society could not survive. But once an institution has persisted for a period past the generation that produced it, men may come to value it as a thing in itself. There is a temptation to regard the temple as fixed, not subject to change. Its devotees come to feel that it is of more significance than the men for whom it exists.

Jesus here declares that the creative, communicative Word of God cannot be contained and confined within any temple. God is always bigger than the institutions that seek to conserve and transmit revelation. For all man's structures are limited and conditioned. At best, they can point toward God—but can never enclose Him.

*. . . every idle word that men shall speak, they shall give account thereof in the day of judgment. For by thy words thou shalt be justified, and by thy words thou shalt be condemned (Matthew 12:36-37).*

Words are not trifles; they are potent and mystical. It is dangerous to take them for granted, to use them carelessly and idly. They are given to us by God in order to perform work—to serve as vehicles for communication of meaning. Any service less than that is a distortion of a divine gift that is an essential and distinguishing trait of mankind. For of all the myriad forms of life on earth, only man has capacity to use words.

32

A word that does no work is like a counterfeit bill; some persons make them and pass them intentionally, while others pass them in ignorance and carelessness. But the damage is comparable in the two situations. However innocently it is passed, the counterfeit is deceptive, empty, hollow, and lacks the potency of a genuine monetary symbol. Circulation of counterfeit bills in any quantity will quickly debase the currency that is imitated.

*And it came to pass, that when Jesus had finished these parables, he departed thence (Matthew 13:53).*

Practically speaking, there comes a time when the warmly urgent message of Jesus is no longer presented to a particular individual. That is, Jesus "leaves" a particular field of work in order to go to another.

An individual deceives himself when he defers decision, assuming that he will always have another chance. For there is a point of view according to which the burden of decision rests upon him. Jesus' pattern of teaching included geographical changes that were too frequent and consistent to be accidental. Always, He offered His message to any who would accept it. But He did not devote His entire ministry to a particular locality or a selected group of individuals.

*At that time Herod the tetrarch heard of the fame of Jesus (Matthew 14:1).*

This is comparatively late in the ministry of Jesus. He has already performed startling miracles. Demon-driven swine have rushed into the sea. Dead men have been raised, and sick ones healed. Great crowds have followed Him about and have talked with eager curiosity about His person and His mission. Yet Herod the tetrarch is just now beginning to get an inkling of what is happening in his own region.

Is not that always the case with men in high places?

To the degree that one is removed from the masses by elevation—whether political or economic or intellectual—understanding and effective communication may be inhibited. Isolation is one of the prices that a man pays for what we call "position." He looks at life through a special set of spectacles that differ widely from those of others on different levels.

Therefore the leader—especially the aloof and self-sufficient and self-consciously elevated leader—is of all men in a group least likely to be informed about what is taking place in the minds of the masses.

*And the king was sorry: nevertheless for the oath's sake, and them which sat with him at meat, he commanded it to be given her (Matthew 14:9).*

Herod was reluctant to order John's death—but was trapped by big talk and social display. In a moment of enthusiasm he boasted before a group of guests—and was not brave enough to confess his mistake. John's martyrdom was a direct result of the fact that a free-handed host tried to win approval of a banquet group by making good on rash blustering.

*And his head was brought in a charger, and given to the damsel: and she brought it to her mother (Matthew 14:11).*

Herodias was the instigator of this monstrous deed. Her supple daughter, whose dancing won the king's promise, was a tool of the older woman. Without denying the reality of individual freedom, we must recognize that parents are usually deeply involved in whatever dreadful deeds are executed by their sons and daughters.

*And his disciples came, and took up the body, and buried it . . . (Matthew 14:12).*

What happened to the head of John? Did his disciples bury it along with the body? Did Herodias keep it as a trophy, or was she quickly sickened by her own successful act of revenge?

34

This head of a prophet, which was a gift made to a woman by a king, can be treated as symbolizing all things coveted. Here, it is the getting that is emphasized; subsequent reactions to the gift are so insignificant that they are not reported. Men may be frantically absorbed in winning a particular prize, without having considered what they will do with it, once it is in hand.

It is well, but very difficult, to stop at intervals and ask: What thing do I most want just now? Precisely why do I want it? What will I do with it if I get it? What will be the significance of success or failure a decade hence?

*. . . he departed thence by ship into a desert place apart . . . (Matthew 14:13).*

How profound was the effect of this withdrawal upon the Saviour's later ministry?

No full answer can be given. This much is certain: His retreat into solitude was charged with emotion at the death of John, and hence was potent in revealing God's will. Sorrow is a powerful lens that bends rays of meaning just as a magnifying glass bends rays of light. A period of solitude for sorrowful meditation can bring a new vision.

Contemporary men too often make the mistake of trying to drown sorrow in activity, rather than using it as a set of spectacles to discover new truth through dedicated searching.

*But when he saw the wind boisterous, he was afraid; and beginning to sink, he cried, saying, Lord, save me (Matthew 14:30).*

Peter's exploit was a self-devised method by which to test his Master. His failure suggests that it is impious and ineffective, as well as dangerous, to test God by any means whatever. The very act of testing implies ability to decide what God can and cannot do; this is a major heresy. Peter's test was doomed to failure, no matter what proof he might have demanded. For there are major

35

differences between seeking proof and accepting in faith that which is beyond proof.

*Then they that were in the ship came and worshipped him, saying, Of a truth thou art the Son of God (Matthew 14:33).*

For the first time, Matthew employs the formula "Son of God" as a title for Jesus. But, though not previously made articulate by the disciples, it cannot have been overlooked. Indeed, walking upon the water is no whit more marvelous than many other events that have already transpired, each of which testified that the worker of mighty works is the Expected One.

Why, then, do the disciples make the exclamation of the text?

Because, in its fullest and deepest sense, the discovery that Jesus of Nazareth is Son of God is progressive. It is not a climactic and all-inclusive discovery of a truth so full-blown that nothing can be added. Rather, encounter with the transforming idea of God-in-the-flesh can take place upon many levels.

Mastery of a really complex idea is like coming to know a person. "Oh, yes, I know Garland Williams," one says after having been casually introduced. But the truth is, this first "knowing" of Garland Williams—though real and valid—is extremely limited. Name and face are recognized, and that is about all. After having been in the congregation when he leads in prayer, the new acquaintance will know him on a higher level. After being with him on a week-end retreat, there is a deeper kind of understanding which can be the basis for exclaiming in a fresh sense, "Yes, I know Garland Williams!"

Just such progressive knowing takes place when one pursues a great idea, gaining deeper understanding of it from each successive encounter.

*. . . his disciples came and besought him, saying, Send her away; for she crieth after us (Matthew 15:23).*

There are few situations more annoying than being pestered

36

by a person who insists upon action already shown to be undesirable or impossible. Jesus had ignored the woman's pleas; by every standard of decorum, that should have been enough. She should have had the good taste to be quiet and go her way.

So when she persisted, the disciples took the natural course of action. They reacted to the problem situation by concluding that there was no solution. When the woman insisted that there was indeed a way out of it, they became impatient and wanted her to leave. So they urged that Jesus dismiss her.

He refused their plea and came up with a radical solution to the woman's problem: the Saviour sent to Israel will heal all who meet the conditions, no matter what their nation or race.

So unexpected an outcome had not occurred to the disciples. Like them, we are prone to treat our problems as insoluble if conventional answers do not fit. Through the Holy Spirit, mere men may find radical new alternatives which constitute undreamed-of solutions to their problems.

*. . . the multitude wondered, when they saw the dumb to speak, the maimed to be whole, the lame to walk, and the blind to see . . . (Matthew 15:31).*

Medical science concentrates on preventing damage and making repairs. Nearly every physical healing is a process which restores one to normalcy or something close to it. This is indeed a source of wonder.

Yet spiritual healing goes beyond this point. Through it a "plus" may be added. One healed is not merely restored to a former state of health; he gains powers not previously held. Hence spiritual healing is far more mysterious and awe-full than is physical healing.

*. . . upon this rock I will build my church; and the gates of hell shall not prevail against it (Matthew 16:18).*

Is hell a closed and barred place, which the church must assault if its barriers are to be broken? Is it the role of the church eternally to take itself into earth's hells, rather than shutting its doors to keep hell from pressing into its own guarded place? Can a church (or congregation) survive—to say nothing of fulfilling its mission—without a ceaseless forward movement into outer edges of some hell?

*. . . Get thee behind me, Satan: thou art an offence unto me: for thou savourest not the things that be of God, but those that be of men (Matthew 16:23).*

It had barely been announced when the church, in the person of Peter its earthly symbol, wished to assure itself of its celestial chief in order to guarantee the new institution against risk.

"Be it far from thee, Lord," (verse 22) says Peter. "Thou savourest not the things that be of God," rejoins his Lord. Here, in a few lines, Matthew has described the history of the church.

At every moment, throughout the centuries, the same drama is repeated; individually and collectively, it is the drama of the possessor.

Jesus confides the church to Peter—for when Peter believes, he is the church. (Every man who believes, in the moment of faith becomes a Peter and a foundation of the church.) But when Peter begins to think of himself as possessor of the good that has been given into his charge, he wishes to administer it as he pleases rather than as it would please the Creator of this good.

Peter will not sanction the running of wild risks; he will hear no talk of killing. He already has his fine ecclesiastical prudence. Order, and not sacrifice, is what he considers good—justice and right are more significant than the extravagance of love. Life, indeed—but not death from which life may be born. The result, but not the condition. . . . For the church leader feels the significance of his institution; his responsibilities are crushing, and he prefers not to risk the treasure which God has committed to him.

38

It is Satan who has whispered the counsel of prudence; in the moment of listening, Peter becomes a personification of the evil one. For the wish to protect the good that is Christ is a sure way to lose it.

*And when the disciples heard it, they fell on their face, and were sore afraid (Matthew 17:6).*

Peter's offer to build three tabernacles is eager and impetuous. The whole idea and the overture belong to him. Rather strangely at first glance, Matthew gives no indication that Peter ever received a formal answer to his offer.

Jesus neither assented nor disagreed. Rather, the proposal suddenly became irrelevant. Peter forgot all about it in the dynamic of a firsthand encounter with God.

That is often the case with the plans of men, whether hastily developed, or harbored for years. When one comes into the presence of the Almighty, values that seemed important and plans that appeared pressing may be instantly forgotten. There is not so much a process of divine refusal as a sudden development that leads to discard of old ideas.

This is a major factor in religious conversion. Coming into vital encounter with the divine, men discard their former values and pursue new ones to the transformation of life.

*. . . O faithless and perverse generation, how long shall I be with you? how long shall I suffer you? . . . (Matthew 17:17).*

This instance of impatience on the part of Jesus is almost without parallel. It is evoked by the inability of His followers to work wonders. How the plodding, colorless church must try the patience of Christ!

A band of persons with vital belief will constantly be doing things that, by all ordinary standards, are impossible. Lacking such performances, one wonders whether a body of worshippers can hope to deserve the approbation of the Master.

*. . . nothing shall be impossible unto you (Matthew 17:20).*

No mental attitude is more inhibiting than a keen sense of what is impossible. Any person who has a neat catalog of the things that can't be attained is a contributor to his own limitations. Acceptance of the culture's list of impossibilities is a way of closing doors. We are too ignorant to know what can't be done in faith, so should avoid mapping precise boundaries beyond which we cannot go.

*. . . Have ye not read, that he which made them at the beginning made them male and female (Matthew 19:4).*

Like all God's gifts, sex has potential for perversion. It is among the dangerous opportunities conferred upon men by a Father who has given us a degree of freedom. But the reality of man's abuse does not affect the nature of the original precious gift.

Sex is conferred by God. It is not an accident, but the fruit of purpose. It has potential for holiness, creativity, co-working with the divine. So it is not to be condemned outright, as in some cultural epochs and in the writings of some men. Rather, the glory and mystery of sex can become subjects for men to ponder. Recognizing its holy marvels is a step toward seeing the grandeur of man and the surpassing glory of his Creator.

*. . . there is none good but one, that is, God . . . (Matthew 19:17).*

This verse teases at the mind. For Jesus' first words in reply to an apparently sincere question do not seem to constitute a direct reply. A casual reading makes them appear almost irrelevant.

Yet the Master's reply is actually directed to the question. It asserts that there is no set of good deeds by which any man can become good. By nature, man is incapable of achieving goodness; that is a citadel too high to be stormed.

This deep lesson is often forgotten in attempts to make Christianity a religion of "social justice." Jesus offers personal re-

40

demption—for men who lack capacity to win goodness by observing codes of conduct.

*When his disciples heard it, they were exceedingly amazed, saying, Who then can be saved? (Matthew 19:25).*

This passage is often treated as a blast at the wealthy. Such a view may include the comforting assurance that the poor and generous are likely to win salvation.

That is far from the heart of the teaching. Exceeding amazement would not have been evoked by condemnation of the occasional man wealthy by the standards of his culture. Rather, astonishment of the disciples comes from the realization that any man who has worldly possessions is rich. That includes everyone, even the monk who owns only the privilege of occupying a particular cell during certain hours of the day.

Everything in the context suggests that Jesus is not simply warning a small per cent of persons who are wealthy by human standards. On the contrary, the Master is saying that no man is capable of winning salvation. It is a state beyond the possibility of achievement. It must come as a gift, not as an earned reward.

Material things handicap the pilgrim; yet he cannot pursue his journey without them. We are caught in the paradoxical state of being liable to condemnation by virtue of relationships we cannot eliminate. Until we recognize the depth of our own plight, we are not candidates for salvation—no matter how eagerly we may strive for achievement in our own strength.

*But Jesus answered and said, Ye know not what ye ask . . . (Matthew 20:22).*

This rebuke is pertinent in most instances of yearning for "greatness." No person seeking it can really know what he is requesting; he will see it from a different perspective when he arrives at the goal. This is inevitable and inescapable. For the "great" man is no longer the same person who longed for prestige and viewed it from a distance. Lord Acton summed up his interpretation of history in one sentence: "Power tends to corrupt; absolute power corrupts absolutely."

The text also warns that it is easy to plunge into frenzied striving for something we wouldn't want if we would take a good look at it.

*. . . Behold, thy King cometh unto thee, meek, and sitting upon an ass . . . (Matthew 21:5).*

There may be great significance in what appears to be trivial. For the Messiah to ride upon a donkey was quite different from entering the city upon a horse. One animal is big, bold, a symbol of strength and pride. The other is meek, small, and humble. Perhaps ancient readers were more sensitive to this matter than are moderns.

What does this say about transportation of today's spiritual leader: minister, church-school teacher, deacon? What impact does make and model of one's automobile have upon others? What are the psychological effects upon the rider from the vehicle (or animal) that transports him? How trivial or how significant an index to the times is our all-but-universal concern for bigger, bolder, newer vehicles—whose role as agents of transportation has become subsidiary to roles in establishing prestige, good taste, and acceptance of cultural values?

*And a very great multitude spread their garments in the way; others cut down branches from the trees, and strawed them in the way (Matthew 21:8).*

Details of a modern parade differ from those of an ancient one. Ticker tape and confetti tend to take the place of garments and branches. Yet there are similarities: large numbers of persons make exuberant demonstrations honoring a person whom they do not know personally.

Almost any parade will attract masses of shouters. Yet the level of encounter is so remote that there is not likely to be any influence upon typical viewers.

To what degree should the church and its institutions engage in staging parades, and to what degree should they be repudiated? No answer can apply to more than a few situations. Always there is the crucial question whether any crowd larger than a self-conscious minority can deserve the name "Christian." Success in attracting masses of shouters is no standard by which to measure the work of an individual or a congregation.

*And they answered Jesus, and said, We cannot tell . . . (Matthew 21:27).*

Men absorbed in self-concern and fearful of damage to their status are great fence-sitters; they adopt the "do not have a judgment" position as a public pose.

Chief priests and elders had clear ideas, but did not care to risk bringing them into the open. Such an attitude is neither conciliation nor delay in order to seek truth. Rather, it is an escape device motivated by self-interest.

*. . . Render therefore unto Caesar the things which are Caesar's; and unto God the things that are God's (Matthew 22:21).*

There is a gulf between "the world" and "the Kingdom." One is material and temporal, the other is spiritual and eternal. There are interconnections between the two realms, of course; but there are no bridges strong enough to bear heavy traffic.

God's sovereignty, though absolute, does not in practice extend to details of such matters as rulers, taxes, and social justice. Man has limited control over these realms; in effect, his mastery of details is complete. God is not concerned with "justice" or "injustice" of the fact that a hillbilly crooner earns $300,000 a year while an old saint shepherding a flock of mountain folk earns $1800 a year.

By paying homage to material success, the pilgrim divides his loyalty. God's Kingdom is wholly nonmaterial, focused beyond time and taxes.

*... The scribes and the Pharisees sit in Moses' seat (Matthew 23:2).*
Few nations produce more than one Moses. It is inevitable that some leaders will be inferior to great pioneers of the past. This social process is as inescapable as up-and-down cycles in patterns of individual lives.

At any time, in the life of any people, it would be possible to survey the situation and become melancholy over the quality of the men who sit in the seat of Moses. One could wail and moan over "how far we have fallen." It would be possible to argue that instead of making progress, society is moving backward.

Yet Jesus does not find this a basis for condemnation or despair. Rather, He upholds the dignity of office on the part of scribes and Pharisees while warning men not to stumble because their leaders fail them.

*But be not ye called Rabbi . . . (Matthew 23:8).*
Social life requires the use of titles; they have a functional role so fundamental it cannot be eliminated.

Yet titles constitute a major source of danger. By placing emphasis upon them, men become arrogant and proud. They claim to have reached a state of knowledge or success that is appropriately indicated by the title. This point of view inhibits growth and precludes the striving that alone leads to new truth.

When a man thinks of himself as a teacher for a period of many years, he may forget to be a learner. That is the danger. A title valued for itself becomes a suit of clothes like those worn by Hans Andersen's emperor. It is transparent, and fails to cover the nakedness of the man who struts under it.

Men cannot get along together in groups without some hierarchy of responsibility and a set of titles to indicate levels. So long as one is conscious of dangers inherent in labels, he is not likely to be greatly hurt by them. When one becomes so comfortable with a title that it no longer sounds a bit strange in his ears, he needs to examine himself earnestly.

*Ye blind guides, which strain at a gnat, and swallow a camel (Matthew 23:24).*

Probably some rough fellows swallowed gnats without hesitation. But the better folk with nice manners were meticulous to get every wee insect out of a vessel before drinking. It is these members of polite religious society, says Jesus, who fail to strain out camels!

So the challenge centers in the question: "What is really important—and what only seems to be important?"

Any man who can find a definitive answer is on the way toward creative life. But, says Jesus, the most pious folk of the religious institution are likely to be equipped with strainers of the wrong mesh. They strain out trifles (which are no trifles to those who make the strainers), but let big things pass.

Most men do honestly want to honor the right goals. In our clumsy way, we try to weave nets to catch the right things. But we lack capacity to do the job; try as we may, we are certain to fail. Only when we accept divine help do we gain capacity to transcend these limitations.

*. . . there shall be weeping and gnashing of teeth (Matthew 24:51).*

This appears to be a strange combination of reactions. Weeping is usually so dominant an activity that it commands one's whole being. Gnashing is associated with rage, not sorrow—at least in today's culture.

Was the connotation different in the first century? If not, then we are faced with the problem that Jesus has the doomed and the damned suffering sorrow and rage simultaneously—which is a way of saying that the torment of rejection by God goes beyond anything we can experience or effectively conceive. Such a description is a pointer toward a condition, rather than a neat formula that contains all elements in the compound. That this is not an accidental combination is indicated by its repetition. See 22:13; 25:30.

*. . . the spirit indeed is willing, but the flesh is weak (Matthew 26:41).*

When emphasis is upon the latter aspect of this appraisal, it may be quoted as a confession of failure and admission of weakness on the part of all men. But weakness of the flesh does not cancel out the altogether thrilling fact that the spirit is willing! Here is a testimony to man's special glory. God has equipped us to engage in struggle which is as real as our inevitable failure; we have capacity to accept ideals we cannot achieve. This is the divine imprint on the creature who is a little lower than the angels.

*. . . O my Father, if this cup may not pass away from me, except I drink it, thy will be done (Matthew 26:42).*

It appears strange that "drinking the cup" should be the only way in which it can be made to pass away. Yet this is true in many crises. When a major tragic decision is faced, deliberate response to it is the sole way in which tension may be relieved. Barring the taking of action, a cup can remain before one indefinitely. Seizure of the cup represents a solution to the dilemma, and the means by which to make it pass away.

*. . . They answered and said, He is guilty of death (Matthew 26:66).*

This verdict represents a clear-cut reaction to the charge of blasphemy. In the name of holiness, men condemn another to death in order to protect God.

However pious they may be, do men ever need to do violence in defending the good name of Jehovah? Does man's abuse of man actually bring honor to the God in whose cause "justice" is done?

Answers to this set of questions have implications that apply to all religious persecutions, passings of judgment, and punishments of men who violate the religious code.

*When he was set down on the judgment seat, his wife sent unto him ... (Matthew 27:19).*

This incident explodes the fallacy according to which women of the first century had no voice in affairs of men!

It was a grave and weighty hour, an occasion of state. Pilate was seated on the official bench of a judge. That is, federal court was in session. All the opening solemnities had been observed. It was no time to deal lightly with customs or to interrupt formal proceedings.

Yet Pilate's wife dared to send him an urgent message!

In this man-dominated world, perhaps we would fare better if wives broke into formal sessions more often and interrupted with greater urgency. How much better would society be if wives of leaders disagreed with their husbands more frequently and vigorously—not only in the home, but also on state occasions? How many rash and cruel judgments would be left unpronounced if men refused to take a major step against the strong opposition of their wives?

*... they bowed the knee before him, and mocked him, saying, Hail, King of the Jews! (Matthew 27:29).*

It is always mockery to worship Jesus as a material king—to deck Him in the symbols of human power, then bow down to Him for the same reasons that courtiers prostrate themselves before princes.

This pretense of paying homage to the Saviour was a case of play-acting by adults. Men went through the forms of worship, bestowed sham symbols of rank. The scarlet robe was the color of royalty. And though plaited of thorns (whose cruel beauty is unsurpassed in nature), the crown still symbolized material

47

power. Even the words of homage were used in mock ceremony.

Perhaps every symbol of power is as empty as the scarlet robe and the crown of thorns. Men do bow down before them. They flex their knees, bow their heads, go through all the motions of reverent appreciation. But all the time, they may actually be despising the man whom they purport to honor. Every dictator and demagogue on any level quickly draws the hatred of those who may be smooth and adept in paying homage to him.

*They gave him vinegar to drink mingled with gall: and when he had tasted thereof, he would not drink (Matthew 27:34).*

This was the most powerful painkiller known; Jesus refused to take it. What does this say to people rushing to buy painkillers and supporting frantic research for more and more powerful ones?

There can be a transforming quality in pain—provided it is accepted as part of God's plan for life. So taken, it forms a pearl instead of a cancer. Instead of an evil to be avoided, it is a blessing to be taken and used for the furtherance of a major goal—no less than that of entry into the Kingdom.

It is perverted to seek pain, to enjoy it in one's life or the lives of others. But it is dangerous to run from pain, to fear it so much that one feels his life will cave in if he experiences great pain. So treated, pain becomes a monster that seems to pursue the victim who flees from it.

More courage and less tranquilizing drugs could help change the complexion of contemporary society.

*And for fear of him the keepers did shake, and became as dead men (Matthew 28:4).*

Some kinds of fear are wholesome. Fear may serve to challenge one to use all his resources, exert his entire strength, pitch enthusiastically into a difficult undertaking. Without such prodding from fear, it is easy to become complacent and to drift—or worse, to become a victim of unholy pride.

But there is a point at which fear ceases to be therapeutic and wholesome. It becomes overpowering, stifling, deadening. It can so dominate thought that the fearful person is "as dead," incapable of showing symptoms of life.

One who is fearful of consequences will never launch a new enterprise. He will never speak up against the crowd. He will not be willing to stand and be counted.

Unless—and this is the cosmic "if"—unless his life-dominating fear is wholly centered in God. That being the case, one can be so fearful of the consequences, spiritually speaking, that he becomes indifferent to material consequences. He is not so much courageous—though he may appear so in the eyes of men—as he is oblivious to the values by which other men live. He does not weigh the consequences, because he is as a dead man with regard to success, prominence, fame, and power.

*And when they saw him, they worshipped him: but some doubted (Matthew 28:17).*

The Great Commission was delivered to a group of men who had actually walked with Jesus—but who were not wholly convinced, even by encounter with their risen Lord. These men, who had doubters among them, were sent with a promise of power—even though they wavered.

The messenger who must have absolute certainty before he accepts a commission may actually tie the hands of God! Sometimes we need to go, even though not certain in logical fashion about all the details of Jesus' life and message; going in doubt, but armed with His commission, the uncertain one who obeys may find power in the act of delivering the message and doing as commanded.

49

BETHEL SEMINARY WEST
LIBRARY
4747 College Avenue
San Diego, California 92115

# THE GOSPEL OF
# Mark

*The voice of one crying in the wilderness ... (Mark 1:3).*

Why should one cry in the wilderness? Perhaps because every true prophet is uncomfortable within a rigid established institution. Though he is the fruit of a social and religious system, he has so radical a break-through into new thought that the old institution cannot contain him. Instead of adapting his message so that it can be proclaimed with comfort and safety in the city, he retreats into an unsettled place and witnesses to those hardy and curious enough to follow him.

*And there went out unto him all the land of Judaea, and they of Jerusalem, and were all baptized ... (Mark 1:5).*

Always, there is magnified potential for radical change when hearers have gone out from familiar patterns to strange new ones. That is one reason for the high ratio of decisions in tents and stadiums. All the stabilizing and restraining influences of the customary are removed.

Part of the task of worship is to induce men to adventure, to go beyond the routine and taken-for-granted, to arrive at a place where they are sufficiently uninhibited to make radical decisions.

*. . . There cometh one mightier than I after me, the latchet of whose shoes I am not worthy to stoop down and unloose (Mark 1:7).*

Every religious leader needs constant awareness of allegiance to God, in whose presence the sense of humility is overpowering. Lacking this, a teacher or elder or pastor tends to become proud, to identify his cause with his own person, to measure his success by the degree to which he draws men to himself.

Unloosing of shoestrings is the act of a menial. So John here reminds us that no witness is of himself good enough to deserve to be a servant of Christ. We serve Him, not because we are better than other men, but because we are more sensitive to our unworthiness than are the indifferent. The instant the servant becomes proud, he loses his dynamic as a witness.

*And immediately the spirit driveth him into the wilderness (Mark 1:12).*

Perhaps without ever having considered why, we are accustomed to thinking of the Spirit as primarily playing the role of leader. We find it easy to talk of being "led by the Spirit," but find something brusque and harsh in the notion of being "driven by the Spirit."

It is an oversight to fail to recognize the driving, goading, and forcing work of God. Men driven by the Spirit into the wilderness do not emerge unchanged. There is no guarantee that they will be better and stronger; they may fail under stress. But the one who has been driven—and not merely led—is changed by the experience.

*And Jesus said unto them, Come ye after me, and I will make you to become fishers of men (Mark 1:17).*

What is the quality of Christianity that makes the convert

become a fisher for others? Part of it stems from the fact that one greatly thrilled by a book, a car, recipe, song, or an original idea is at once eager to share and socialize the discovery. This applies to most areas of life, not religion only. But the thrill of a discovery in any area is likely to wear off quickly. To keep his zeal and dynamic, the fisherman must keep fishing—and catching! Only continuous personal striving, growing, and discovering can keep an evangelist contagious rather than professional.

*And there was in their synagogue a man with an unclean spirit; and he crieth out (Mark 1:23).*

Because the church is made up of men who do not shake off their human limitations, it always includes some who are possessed by evil spirits. Hence any entering of Christ into a religious assembly is likely to evoke an outcry and a demand for His departure.

*... I know thee who thou art, the Holy One of God (Mark 1:24).*

It is highly interesting that, over and over, the demon-possessed recognize Jesus' divinity while ordinary folk remain blind to it. Why is it that the odd one, the eccentric should so consistently and repeatedly figure here? Aside from problems linked with dualism (recognition of the benign superhuman by the demonic superhuman) there remains the fact that a really well-adjusted person, comfortable in all the conventional grooves of the culture, may actually be less qualified to see and recognize divine intrusion than a person who leans toward the bizarre. One can be so very comfortable and conventional that a person-to-person confrontation by the divine leads to nothing more than a raised eyebrow. (See Mark 3:12.)

*... what new doctrine is this? ... (Mark 1:27).*

There is no hint of preaching or formal teaching in connection with the healing that evokes so much astonishment and comment.

Yet men find in the situation the conclusion that "here is a man with a new message."

Inevitably, deeds and formal teachings are inseparable; to succeed in doing strange or remarkable things is a way to spread a new doctrine. We teach in all our acts, even those that seem most removed from anything like formal exhortation. Teaching is not something set apart into one compartment; it is an activity that pervades all. Every man teaches every hour.

*. . . they held their peace (Mark 3:4).*

There is silence that stems from uncertainty, suspended judgment, open-mindedness. And there is silence from unwillingness to take sides, stand and be counted. Here the events clearly indicate that the latter factors prevailed. One of life's most difficult problems centers in the question of when to be silent and when to speak—and it is not easy to be sure of one's own motives even.

*And unclean spirits, when they saw him, fell down before him, and cried, saying, Thou art the Son of God (Mark 3:11).*

Unclean spirits witness to God incarnate, while leading lights of the congregation watch suspiciously, seeking a basis for accusation and condemnation! Almost, it seems that genuine conversion requires some degree of aloofness from an established system, or some degree of break with it. Fierce defense of an inherited system—even one that employs the Christian vocabulary—usually produces intellectual complacency and religious bigotry.

*And when his friends heard of it, they went out to lay hold on him . . . (Mark 3:21).*

Well-intentioned friends can be a man's worst enemies. They can put blockades in his path in a way impossible to strangers or foes. Breaking with the gang, the cocktail crowd, the old cronies, may be one of the most difficult steps in a spiritual adventure.

54

Friends resist actively, try to hold the one "beside himself" within the conventional pattern—and they do it for the sake of what they sincerely consider his own best interest.

*There came then his brethren and his mother, and, standing without, sent unto him, calling him (Mark 3:31).*

In many types of estrangement, ranging from family squabbles and intellectual debates to community schisms and denominational rivalry, men seek to be reconciled with their opponents by standing outside and calling them. Part of this reaction is due to pride and stubbornness. Perhaps part of it is due to fear of being convinced from vital personal encounter. There are few situations where mutual yielding would fail to bring harmony, if antagonists could be brought into real meeting and two-way communication. Here, mother and brothers would have changed their views had they gone inside to talk with Jesus rather than standing outside and calling Him.

*... Who is my mother, or my brethren? (Mark 3:33).*

For Jesus, every event is the springboard for a profound question. He takes no ideas for granted, but jolts minds by turning light on unnoticed facets of the universally accepted. For Him, everything has religious implications and can cast light on the all-absorbing matter of His message and mission. To ask such a question about what seems obvious is far more difficult than to engage in exotic travel or research along the fringes of knowledge.

*... there was gathered unto him a great multitude, so that he entered into a ship, and sat in the sea ... (Mark 4:1).*

It is the mood of the modern church to be eager for crowds—the bigger they are, the better. But notice that the very mechanical nature of a crowd poses problems. Here, Jesus is forced to increase the separation between Himself and His audience by the size of the group. Success in attracting large crowds is sure to bring with it some new problems.

*And the cares of this world, and the deceitfulness of riches, and the lusts of other things entering in, choke the word . . . (Mark 4:19).*

This trilogy can hardly have been chosen accidentally, or even casually. All three preoccupations are aspects of ego-involvement. All three focus in material and temporal values. Persons who concentrate on such matters will thereby crowd out concern for non-material goals.

To transcend preoccupation with bodily wants is the grand spiritual struggle. Continuous radical transformations, or breaks in the patterns of material striving, are essential. Worldliness is as easy to espouse in pulpit or monastery as in a bank.

*. . . Take heed what ye hear: with what measure ye mete, it shall be measured to you . . . (Mark 4:24).*

Every occasion for hearing is a testing ground for the hearer. It is as though free milk were being given out, in bulk. Every man who comes will receive as much as he can carry away. One man wheels in a twenty-gallon drum; another carries a five-gallon can on his shoulder. Behind him is a fellow with a paper cup in his hand. Each gets as much as he can take away; with the measure he measures, it is measured out to him.

The "measure" is the total self in its capacity for encounter with or seizure of meaning in any event. To the blind, the world is literally without light. One's passing of judgment upon a person or message is a most effective standard by which to judge the analyst. Here is a man who honestly thinks the Sistine Chapel is ugly; that not only says something about his soul—it also measures him, in the sense that his own limitations determine what he can receive from a visit to a masterpiece.

*But when the fruit is brought forth, immediately he putteth in the sickle, because the harvest is come (Mark 4:29).*

This deep parable is a kind of commentary on the doctrine expressed above, especially in verse 25. On human and materialistic terms the comment is almost as obscure as the teaching it illuminates. For man is the wheat; if he is to be cut down as soon as he bears fruit, why bother?

Because man's meaning is not exhausted in himself. Because material notions of "justice" are not so much wrong as irrelevant. They apply only within history; here we are dealing with cosmic values.

Divine judgment is often treated in a purely negative fashion. Actually, it is a positive process. Fruit-bearing is a means of fulfillment by God and garnering in His barns; barrenness produces nothing for Him to harvest.

*. . . Whereunto shall we liken the kingdom of God? or with what comparison shall we compare it? (Mark 4:30).*

Common sense suggests that a most exalted comparison is necessary.

Yet Jesus finds comparisons in the most simple and familiar of events. If the Kingdom is marvelous, and if simple things really do point to it, then it follows that all simple things are actually marvelous—if only we find eyes to discover how very wonderful they are!

*It [the kingdom] is like a grain of mustard seed . . . (Mark 4:31).*

Interpretation usually centers on the marvelous growth from tiny to huge. That is a valid view, but it is not the heart of the matter.

No one can say why a tiny seed should produce a big plant, when some big seeds yield small plants. Logic is transcended. There is mystery here. It is beyond man's bundling into neat packages of knowledge. The riddle is bigger than the man who studies it.

Just so, the Kingdom grows in ways that no man can fathom. Committees on evangelism try to reduce the mystery to a turnover chart and a set of easily mastered techniques. Usually they succeed only in magnifying man while oversimplifying God and hence worshipping an idol.

*. . . Why are ye so fearful? how is it that ye have no faith? (Mark 4:40).*

This miracle says that faith drives out fear, even physical fear of the most acute type. But there is more here. The fear of the disciples was rooted in their concern for themselves. They have already shown a degree of what we are tempted to call petulance (verse 38). It is most inconsiderate of the Master to lie there sleeping, no matter how weary He may be, when they are in danger. He is not afraid; He knows nothing of the high waves and the storm. But if He really cared about them (they reason), He would not lie there sleeping but would rise and show His concern.

Here, as in most or all other instances, fear is rooted in the ego. It is linked with self-concern. For the person who is fully absorbed in a goal outside the self is thereby cut off from fear. He doesn't have time or energy to devote to worry about himself. His one concern is for the goal to which he has given himself. Hence he can face waves or lions or boards of directors without so much as one tremor.

*. . . What have I to do with thee, Jesus, thou Son of the most high God? I adjure thee by God, that thou torment me not (Mark 5:7).*

Men possessed by evil spirits may resist their deliverer and reproach him for cruelty. No matter how fearful they may be, a man who has lived with his demons for years is likely to be so attached to them that he dislikes the prospect of losing them. Courage and radical cures are required if one would be of help to the desperate.

58

*. . . Go home to thy friends, and tell them how great things the Lord hath done for thee . . . (Mark 5:19).*

Often, a great act of healing challenges the recipient, not to do the dramatic by leaving for far-off places, but to accept the much more difficult assignment of staying at home to witness among friends and relatives. This is probably the hardest, as well as the most vital, kind of witnessing.

*And he departed, and began to publish in Decapolis how great things Jesus had done for him . . . (Mark 5:20).*

His cure restored the man to society. He was moved to turn from the tombs to the town. This was literally an act of taming (verse 4). When a man can be transformed from the self-centeredness of solitary madness to public witness about his own healing, he has rejoined society. It is true that only those who themselves have been mad will fully understand his testimony. But he is no longer a solitary one; he is a fully human member of organized society.

*. . . Be not afraid, only believe (Mark 5:36).*

This formula sounds "too simple." It may even be considered a naïve exhortation.

That is precisely its grandeur. It *is* too simple in the eyes of men who doubt and fear and demand reasonable explanations. For the miracle is much more than simply a demonstration of power over death. It says that for one who believes, it never is too late! (See verse 35.) In our human limitations we surrender too soon, failing to recognize that our concepts do not bind God. Faith operates to sever the bonds of "impossibility" with which we have tied our own hands.

*And he suffered no man to follow him, save Peter, and James, and John . . . (Mark 5:37).*

Some of the highest and most solemn of miracles must be

worked in places where the curious do not throng. We make a mistake to limit the dynamic of God to the public service of evangelism and to the crowded altar. Under some conditions and in relation to some personalities, a small group of genuinely concerned folk may be more conducive to reception of the Holy Spirit than would be the case with a mass of the curious and enthusiastic.

*And he cometh to the house of the ruler of the synagogue, and seeth the tumult, and them that wept and wailed greatly (Mark 5:38).*

Much of our individual and group weeping and wailing is premature. We assume finality in the light of our own best knowledge, whereas no human understanding is decisive or final in the event of fresh encounter with divine power.

We assume the worst, worry, and weep. Worse, we laugh in superior knowledge at any messenger who dares suggest that God can crash through those barriers that men consider insuperable. One who centers his attention on the mystery and might of God, sure of being held in His hand, has neither time nor energy to wail.

*. . . they were astonished with a great astonishment (Mark 5:42).*

The gospel writers see no limit to human capacity for astonishment. There is no indication that they feel readers might become surfeited with wonders and begin to take them for granted. On the contrary, it is clear that the evangelists believe each fresh encounter with the Saviour can be an occasion for amazement.

Capacity for wonder grows rather than shrinks. A man who finds it hard to wonder at anything will shrug aside an earth-shaking miracle. One who has cultivated wonder, especially wonder at the work of our Lord, can see a miracle in any event.

If ten men have been healed of leprosy, it creates a situation in which it is easy to regard the cure as established and to shrug

60

off the eleventh cure as commonplace. According to the viewpoint of the gospel writers, the eleventh cure is no less remarkable, no less earth-shaking, no less a source of marvel and praise than is the first cure. Much of our thin, empty living results from inability to treat the millionth occurrence of a miracle as being equal in rank to the first instance of it. (See 7:37.)

*And he charged them straitly that no man should know it . . . (Mark 5:43).*

Publicity is forbidden; a miracle is to be hidden!

For the sake of the child healed, who might become a curiosity or a freak. . . .

For the sake of the healer's mission, already jeopardized by masses of the bored and the curious and others who have no understanding of the message but who, by their great number, even tempt those of the inner circle to magnify "success" features of the movement. . . .

For the sake of seekers, who will eagerly throng to Jesus for mere physical healing, and be bitterly disappointed that no miracle is worked for them—that their dead mother is not lifted from the grave, that the horde of gold hidden somewhere on the farm in disturbances of the Maccabaean Wars goes undiscovered, that the Messiah does not choose to wave His hand and drive out the Roman conqueror.

*. . . And they were offended at him (Mark 6:3).*

Some of our most belligerent instances of taking offense are linked with the wounded pride that stems from startling confrontation with the strange, illogical, and unreasonable. Men bewildered by a proposal for new labor laws, or a new hypothesis of the solar system, or the incredible demonstration that a white man has dynamic love for a black-skinned brother, may salve the wounded ego by fierce attacks upon the author of the disturbance. So whenever one finds himself actively hating another for what he symbolizes, it is time to engage in serious soul-searching to find the real cause for the offense.

*. . . A prophet is not without honour, but in his own country . . . (Mark 6:4).*

This is a profound analysis, not simply of community ways, but of the nature of human knowledge.

That which is known, accepted, granted by the community, may loom so large in one's system of thought that the rearrangement attendant upon assimilating a new aspect of the known is literally impossible. Hence, a novice or a stranger may be more receptive to radical insight than is a veteran. This is one of the curses of professionalism, in religion as much as any other area. This is part of the "hardening" of the Hebrews. It is an aspect of the "body of death" shackled to the soul that could proceed toward the Eternal City with great speed, were it not burdened with heritages from the past.

*And he marvelled because of their unbelief . . . (Mark 6:6).*

Unbelief is not lack of a system of belief; everyone has that by necessity, if he functions as a sane member of society. Rather, unbelief in any particular instance is an effect of allegiance to a competitive set of "certainties" that resist and inhibit new faith. Total skepticism would result in a state of insanity or incoherence. Men cannot choose whether or not they will believe; they can only choose what they will believe.

*. . . In what place soever ye enter into an house, there abide till ye depart from that place (Mark 6:10).*

This is a subsidiary aspect of absolute commitment. Men who truly serve a life-absorbing idea can't afford to fritter their time and energy in seeking such trivial things as a softer bed, cleaner room, better menu, more congenial hosts or fellow guests. One who devotes his energies to such matters is taking away from his own accomplishments. He elevates minor things to first place—even if on a temporary basis. At best, he reduces his impact; at worst, he becomes restless and querulous to the point of impotence.

*And whithersoever he entered, into villages, or cities, or country, they laid the sick in the streets, and besought him that they might touch if it were but the border of his garment . . . (Mark 6:56).*

The sick were consistently laid in the market places—centers of community activity—by their friends and relatives. This underscores the importance of recognizing social elements in the cure of the sick individual. Frequently a person has reached a state in which he is no longer capable of voluntarily going where he may encounter the divine messenger and find healing. If he is to make contact, someone must take him.

In many instances, healing will take place only after friends of a sick man have volunteered their help: "Let us take you to the Master. He can restore you. We'll make the healing possible by putting you in a place where you can touch Him." It is part of the Master's challenge that those who are well should bestir themselves to bring the sick to clinics they would never attend without urging and help.

*. . . in vain do they worship me, teaching for doctrines the commandments of men (Mark 7:7).*

This quotation from Isaiah strikes at the heart of many problems of tradition, doctrine, and ritual. No matter how exalted a human precept may be, it is conditioned by the humanity of those who make it public. Though wholly committed to God, whom he would serve as messenger, the human witness can only transmit revelation in terms that his contemporaries can grasp.

Men therefore make a fundamental mistake when they seize upon the externals of a message—words, gestures, ways of dress, ceremonial—and begin to treat them as though they were the center of meaning. Precepts of men are elevated to the status of doctrines delivered by God, not subject to change or analysis. Instead of seeking the God to whom precepts can only point, men focus their eyes upon keeping the delivered commandments. They sincerely believe they are worshipping Jehovah, but actually do nothing more than venerate man-shaped precepts that came into being as pointers toward Jehovah.

*For from within, out of the heart of men, proceed evil thoughts, adulteries, fornications, murders, Thefts, covetousness, wickedness, deceit, lasciviousness, an evil eye, blasphemy, pride, foolishness (Mark 7:21-22).*

There is a sense in which evil is but a choice of less than the best. But that view does not exhaust the matter.

Here, Mark offers a terse report of Jesus' analysis of evil as something essentially positive. It has real being in itself, and is not simply an absence of the good. Almost, the passage seems to say that man secretes evils just as he manufactures bile and perspiration. He is so constituted that the normal, routine operation of his total self results in constant production of evils. They come from within and are made by man—and are not simply outside issues that he may confront or side-step.

According to such a view, man can no more escape producing evil than he can escape ejecting carbon dioxide when he breathes. It is a condition of life which he did not create, but which requires his reckoning. Perhaps this is close to the heart of a New Testament doctrine of original sin—obscured by the fact that men take precepts of the past, such as the story of Adam's fall, and transform them into doctrines. Such inherited doctrines may be revered in such fashion that they no longer point to a divine truth which they are too small to inclose (see verse 7). So the dreadful reality of the human limitedness that is "original sin" and the source of inescapable evil, becomes obscured by argument over formulas to describe it.

*And he looked up, and said, I see men as trees, walking (Mark 8:24).*

This pattern of reaction is without parallel in the gospel story. It says, at least, that even a firsthand encounter with Jesus by a person blind in sin and ignorance does not lead to a standard, stereotyped result. For Jesus heals total personalities. Goals, guilts, emotions, memories, and hopes are involved—and vary from one blind man to another. Hence the act of healing must proceed within a complex system of relationships, not a personality vacuum. To insist on uniformity in the rite of healing or its results is to deny the significance of individuals who come seeking to have their eyes opened.

*. . . the father of the child cried out, and said with tears, Lord, I believe; help thou mine unbelief (Mark 9:24).*

This poignant cry helps distinguish between vital belief and the mere formal acceptance of dogmatism and the authoritarian stream of religion. For faith is a state of fear and trembling, longing and growth. It lacks the rigidity and complacency that mark mere orthodoxy. One may be the soul of orthodoxy without ever having experienced growth-inducing faith. Belief with no questions and tears, all tied up neatly in a package, becomes dead dogmatism.

*But they understood not that saying, and were afraid to ask him (Mark 9:32).*

Are these disciples dummies or small boys? Of course not! We look through twentieth-century eyes when we condemn or patronize them in such instances as this. Our humanizing of Jesus —carried to the extent of favoring "sweet" portraits—obscures the fact that the Saviour, to be a real Saviour, must to a degree be one who is feared, misunderstood, and regarded with wonder and awe. There are times when even the most intimate dare not ask explanations. Divine personality is not to be fully penetrated or comprehended. True worship sometimes commands silence.

*For this cause shall a man leave his father and mother, and cleave to his wife; And they twain shall be one . . . (Mark 10:7-8).*

Mutual yielding of self is the central aspect of marriage. It is the most difficult and most enriching aspect of union. It is the key to divorce, which follows when mates so guard the self that they remain two. And it is the key to enlargement of self when borders are broken and each self so flows into the other that both are enlarged in achieving the new unity.

*. . . One thing thou lackest . . . (Mark 10:21).*

It is not to be concluded that the thing lacking is an overt act —but rather, the scale of values out of which the specified act would come spontaneously as a fruit. Charity, even when notable and sacrificial, can be practiced as a technique rather than as a natural accompaniment of a set of values and goals. Spontaneous giving to others does not constitute the heart of Christianity. This practice is only the surface outcropping that points to much deeper veins of dedication. To lack the "one thing" of self-surrender is to lack all.

*. . . with God all things are possible (Mark 10:27).*

This is one of the most thoroughly radical, as well as one of the most difficult, of all gospel teachings. We tend to read it, auto-matically edited, in a form such as: "God is able to do all the things of which man can think, hope and dream. There is no known phenomenon or process that is beyond the power of the Creator."

But such a diluted version is not even close to the meaning of Jesus. He is saying that God can and does act to bring about results so exalted that man cannot incorporate them into his limited systems of thought. They belong on a realm that is not relatively above the human—but absolutely. There is no ladder by which man may climb up to grasp them, regardless of the effort he may exert. God is absolutely and entirely above man's grasp. Hence to ask of Him only that which seems to be reasonable is to limit the work of providence.

*And they shall mock him, and shall scourge him, and shall spit upon him . . . (Mark 10:34).*
In some respects, a cross is easier to accept than spit. Men can die radiantly, when it remains hard to forgive a selfish and complaining neighbor. Not all men can ascend Calvary to become martyrs—but all may emulate the Master in extending forgiveness after the grating, soul-shaking humiliation of being spit upon.

*And many charged him that he should hold his peace: but he cried the more a great deal . . . (Mark 10:48).*
Violation of cultural codes, even to the point of exhibiting frightfully bad manners, may be a major factor in the quest for a cure. So long as one is content to stay within conventional boundaries, willing to be brought up short by an obstacle that men consider absolute, there is no transcending it in a break-through into new life.

Tradition, in the largest sense, is both the base on which all novelty must rest and the most formidable barrier to achievement of a miracle. In one way or another, men who know the answers (facts, customs, formulas) are always saying, "No, no!" It is only those who refuse to hold their peace who succeed in breaking through to an encounter with the divine.

*Blessed be the kingdom of our father David, that cometh in the name of the Lord: Hosanna in the highest (Mark 11:10).*
This is the key to the mood of the Triumphal Entry. Men hail a king, president, general, or other leader because he symbolizes a complex set of ideas, wants, and convictions of the shouters. When

the leader "fails" in whatever fashion—that is, does not establish a system whose effects on the shouters are as wanted and expected —then repudiation is the only alternative to radical change on the part of those who shouted.

Savagery of demands for crucifixion is the logical denouement when masses find they have cheered a leader who stands for something different from that which the followers want. This is the paradox of leadership. Masses never elevate leaders for the most sublime reasons; the man who is better than his supporters is not likely to be "successful" even so long as he who is not so good as his followers.

*. . . Jesus went into the temple, and began to cast out them that sold and bought in the temple, and overthrew the tables of the moneychangers, and the seats of them that sold doves (Mark 11:15).*

Every human institution or custom, no matter how good it may be in its original form, contains within it the possibility of distortion and perversion. It is inherent in the nature of man and his social structures that anything whatever can become treated as an end in itself rather than as a means toward a higher end. Selling of pigeons was originally a convenience for worshippers, as was the availability of coins. But men of low goals saw in these practices a possibility for profit, so they distorted their basic character.

Over and over, individuals and cultures need to ask the double question: Where are we really trying to go—and why? Where are our values really centered; what is it that we are actually— not ostensibly—trying to do? For individual as well as for institution, perhaps the greatest of all failures is to think one is pursuing a high goal, while he is actually absorbed in a very low one.

*. . . no man after that durst ask him any question (Mark 12:34).*
Why should any man fear to ask a question of Jesus?

One answer centers in the fact that many persons do not wish to be disturbed by the explanation that a question will evoke. They prefer to remain in the comfortable state where there seem no enormous, life-shaking, unanswered riddles. For in the incident that led to this climax, Jesus did not offer a clear, precise blueprint. Rather, He challenged the questioner to keep on seeking. Genuine questions tend to move in this direction. Even though they may bring answers, those answers become advance bases from which to project new and more difficult questions.

In a sense, it is a temptation to become more absorbed with answers than with questions. When a person "has the answers," whether on a quiz show or as a specialist in some area of work, we doff the hat to him. As individuals, most of us rather pride ourselves in being able to answer—with firm assurance—some questions raised by a member of the family. But perhaps a more fruitful attitude would be to cultivate the art of asking questions that cannot be met with stereotyped answers.

*. . . Beware of the scribes, which love to go in long clothing . . .
(Mark 12:38).*
This warning raises the whole question of religious symbolism in dress. There are arguments on both sides of the question. Here, however, Jesus doesn't condemn wearing clericals, but the wearer's attitude of adopting that garb in order to get certain results that accrue from it. Given a different motive, the wearing would have different meaning. Display of a cross pinned on one's clothing may be a mere imitative device, or it may represent the fruit of deep religious experience.

*And Jesus saith unto him, Verily I say unto thee, That this day, even in this night, before the cock crow twice, thou shalt deny me thrice (Mark 14:30).*
Much more is involved than a single instance of defection. Peter is the type of humanity; he represents all men, plays the part of

stand-in for every Christian. For, though devoted in principle, he failed in what seemed minor instances—and in the moment of failure did not recognize it as such. Each of us literally denies our Lord three times each day; unlike Peter, we seldom hear the cock crow and recognize our denial, to repent in tears.

*But go your way, tell his disciples and Peter . . . (Mark 16:7).*

It is rather strange to set Peter apart here. Notice that this is Mark's first mention of Peter since his denial. When we last heard of him, he was weeping bitterly. Perhaps it is not unreasonable to think he may have so reproached himself that he wandered away from the band, regarding himself as a hopeless failure. The angel specifies that Peter—the failure—is included in the message. Perhaps this says that when we make especially great mistakes, God is then more concerned than ever to send messages to us.

# THE GOSPEL OF
# Luke

*But the angel said unto him, Fear not Zacharias: for thy prayer is heard; and thy wife Elisabeth shall bear thee a son . . . (Luke 1:13).*

The question of "when" prayer is answered is as real as that of "whether." This account certainly gives the impression that Zacharias and Elisabeth had long ago ceased to pray for a baby. If so, this was not a recent prayer that was being answered.

Fortunately, they were not so old that they were sorry to have a son. But there could be instances when we would be very sorry to have a prayer answered after thirty years—or in some instances, thirty days. So we need to ask whether we pray for things that are hinged to the moment; if we can't have them now, we don't want them. How much better it is to pray for those good things that have no strict temporal attachments, and would be received with joy after many years' delay!

*And he shall go before him in the spirit and power of Elias, to turn the hearts of the fathers to the children, and the disobedient to the wisdom of the just; to make ready a people prepared for the Lord (Luke 1:17).*

It seems entirely usual and normal to think of a great prophet as working to turn the disobedient toward divine wisdom. But it sounds strangely out of place to suggest that in order to make a people ready for the Lord, hearts of fathers must be turned toward the childhood state. It would seem more logical to stress "turning juvenile delinquents toward solid citizens." Perhaps we have underestimated the depth and difficulty of grasping all that is involved in the recurrent gospel challenge to become "like children."

*And the people waited for Zacharias, and marvelled that he tarried so long in the temple (Luke 1:21).*

Every rite and ceremony can become commonplace and conventional to such a degree that any deviation from the customary is a cause of raised eyebrows, wagging tongues. Ritual has lost much vitality when men no longer expect a ceremony to produce unexpected results. When one can be absolutely sure that a service will be dismissed at 11:50, every Sunday of every year, it is time to be jolted out of complacency by a vision from the Lord.

*And when she saw him, she was troubled at his saying, and cast in her mind what manner of salutation this should be (Luke 1:29).*

An initial encounter with a messenger of God may produce more bewilderment than certainty. End results are not evident in first meetings with angels. To expect to know God's will for us—instantly and in complete detail—is presumptuous. There must be response, growth, questions, and answers.

72

*And Mary said, Behold the handmaid of the Lord; be it unto me according to thy word ... (Luke 1:38).*

The marvelous beauty of this incident is dulled by familiarity. Gospel writers were keenly conscious of implications involved in having a baby conceived during a girl's engagement. Mary's response was a token of her complete dedication—even to the point of accepting the label "harlot." Her radiant role could be considered a fruit of passive piety; she was willing to let God work through her—which is not equivalent to a religion of activism and do-goodism.

*And blessed is she that believed: for there shall be a performance of those things which were told her from the Lord (Luke 1:45).*

God makes no one-way promises; all are conditional. Because human freedom is real, we must take a real part in accepting and using God's good gifts. Hence, a divine promise may be "true" for one person and "false" for another—depending upon attitudes and actions of the persons involved. God's performances are reserved for those who believe in His promises.

*And her neighbours and her cousins heard how the Lord had shewed great mercy upon her; and they rejoiced with her (Luke 1:58).*

Cultural emphases of that epoch made it a source of shame for a woman to die without bringing a son into the world. With that passionate yearning for parenthood no longer universal, friends and neighbors of this epoch tend to marvel and titter at the fact that an old man and woman can become a father and mother. Some tend to take it for granted that "young adults" can be partners with God in creating new life. But whether in one's twenties or sixties, parenthood is a sublime mystery. Everyday miracles of the family and home are more stupendous than any wonders of the atomic age—provided we develop capacity to see them as glorious and incredible.

*. . . they were sore afraid (Luke 2:9).*

Holy fear has been too much minimized in modern times. It can be perverted by overemphasis. But it can also be minimized so that the full grandeur of God, and the creaturehood of man, become empty concepts. Over and over, gospel incidents suggest that acute terror accompanies any firsthand encounter with the divine. It is a mistake to linger in fear, but an equally big one to seek deep things of the spirit without a tinge of fright.

*Glory to God in the highest, and on earth peace . . . (Luke 2:14).*

Perhaps there are many varieties of peace. They range from passive submission and lack of interest to that peace which is active and striving, growing and searching. It is a mistake to try to retreat into an easy and colorless peace—a type that, once achieved, becomes a habit. A valid kind of peace must be linked with conscious giving of glory to God. Hence it stems from continuous striving without ever quite arriving. Note that the "peace" which the angels sang about was not physical and material; the entire career of the Babe whom they hailed was intimately linked with trouble, violence, and problems.

*. . . [Anna] was a widow of about fourscore and four years, which departed not from the temple, but served God with fastings and prayers night and day (Luke 2:37).*

Eighty-four years young! Still among the leaders in grasping a radical new idea, still actively seeking and searching!

Here is a creative solution to the problem of use of time by the aged. Anna makes no demand for entertainment; she doesn't even ask for a companion. She has a divine companion who never wearies of conversation. So for her there is no such thing as a problem of what to do with herself. She never has a dull moment, for day and night she is engaged in the most fascinating of all pursuits: a fervent search for God.

74

*. . . after three days they found him in the temple . . . (Luke 2:46).*

Here is a lost boy in a big city. Whether he deliberately stayed behind or was accidentally left is not indicated; the latter seems to be the sense of the passage. If a typical boy were left behind in your city, where would he be attracted: to the pin-ball machine, the pool room, the movie house? What is the modern church doing to make herself attractive to "lost boys"?

*Annas and Caiaphas being the high priests, the word of God came unto John the son of Zacharias in the wilderness (Luke 3:2).*

Judged by ordinary criteria, this seems a highly unlikely time for the word of God to come to anyone. Tiberius Caesar was ruler; the vacillating Pontius Pilate governed Judea; the perfidious Annas and Caiaphas headed the official religious institution of Israel. Men within that system who had sensitive souls doubtless considered the epoch to symbolize hopeless depravity. Yet it was in just such a time that God spoke in a special way through a most unconventional messenger—who was outside the official religious system. God is not limited to picking men from within or without the system; He used both the priest Zacharias and his far-from-priestly son, John. He spoke to Zacharias in the temple and to John in the wilderness. Possibilities of dialogue are unlimited; God can speak anywhere, any time.

*Being forty days tempted of the devil . . . (Luke 4:2).*

Surely there is more than symbolic meaning in the locale of the three temptations that beset the Saviour: wilderness, worldly empire, and temple. Perhaps this strange trio say to us that there is no place whatever, in the physical sense, where one may flee from the devil and be safe from his temptations. Each and every place is vulnerable. Empire is an obvious place of danger; wilderness and temple are not. There is no physical haven into which one may retreat and lock the door; safety can be found only in a spiritual hiding place.

*And he closed the book, and he gave it again to the minister, and sat down . . . (Luke 4:20).*

Having been handed the book of Isaiah's prophecy (verse 17), Jesus unrolled the sheepskin until He found the place He wanted; that is, He selected the Scripture to be interpreted.

To select is also to reject. Only by choosing a few specific goals is it possible to work toward any; the person who tries to do everything will end by doing nothing. One must choose a specific passage, read, and take his seat.

*And in the synagogue there was a man, which had a spirit of an unclean devil . . . (Luke 4:33).*

Physical presence in a holy place is no guarantee against possession by an evil spirit. That is simply a way of saying that members of a congregation remain human—with all the limitations and capacities implied in humanity. It is not a cause for alarm and dismay to find human traits in church folk; this condition is natural and inevitable.

*. . . And when the devil had thrown him in the midst, he came out of him, and hurt him not. And they were all amazed . . . (Luke 4:35-36).*

The process of getting rid of devils is likely to be violent and startling. It is indeed an occasion for amazement when one's personal demons are driven out without lasting injury. So it is essential that the church include in its program some occasions that foster high emotional responses; these may be necessary in order to permit some individuals to boot out their devils.

*. . . he said unto Simon, Launch out into the deep, and let down your nets for a draught (Luke 5:4).*

Are we playing around in safe, shallow water—when we can only make a worthy draught by going into the dangerous depths?

76

*And Simon answering said unto him, Master, we have toiled all the night, and have taken nothing: nevertheless at thy word I will let down the net (Luke 5:5).*

There are occasions when obedience must take priority over understanding. In some instances, men must act without knowing the full explanation for what they are told to do. When a catastrophe threatens, the cry "Run for your life!" bids for action rather than comprehension. This principle has important implications for both Christian education and everyday morality.

*. . . they inclosed a great multitude of fishes: and their net brake (Luke 5:6).*

In fishing for men, too big a haul is dangerous. There is a limit to the effective size of congregations and classes. During an evangelistic enterprise, an overwhelming catch may leave an insuperable problem of assimilation. All "success" is actually limited; carried beyond reasonable limits, any success threatens failure.

*And when they could not find by what way they might bring him in because of the multitude, they went upon the housetop, and let him down through the tiling . . . (Luke 5:19).*

What a completely bold and unconventional thing to do! It involved risking the anger of the man whose roof was torn open, as well as the boos of the crowd. Too often, we quit when obvious and conventional approaches fail. We take the pressure of a multitude as a final and absolute barrier. But religious faith can be channelled toward unconventional solutions to life-absorbing questions. When that is the case, the stage is set for a major miracle.

*And they were all amazed, and they glorified God . . . (Luke 5:26).*

This combination of reactions is by no means automatic or

inevitable. Some folk pass over the unusual, especially that which is apparently commonplace. Others see it but insist upon a rational, scientific explanation—their minds balk at the notion of the inexplicable. Inevitably, those who are blind and those who frame neat explanations have no cause to break into praise of God.

It is only those who see God as the ground out of which all created things come, who move to praise from encounter with a miracle.

*And Levi made him a great feast in his own house . . . (Luke 5:29).*

From the viewpoint of the sanctimoniously pious, this is a strange incident that is quite out of character in the mission of the Son of God.

Levi, the gross man of the world, is won to the fellowship of Jesus. So his first act is to give an expensive party to which he invites those friends whom he knew in his life as a tax collector. And Jesus not only fails to rebuke him; Jesus actually attends!

All sorts of objections could be raised: Levi should have used that money for charity; Levi should have brought his old comrades to Jesus instead of having Jesus come to them; Levi should have made a clean break with his old life and turned his back upon it entirely.

Aside from the fact that this incident indicates a large and kindly tolerance on the part of the Master, it suggests that no one set of procedures is valid for every case of a transformed life. If it is wrong to insist that Levi should have cut off from his old associates upon meeting Jesus, it is equally wrong to insist that every new convert should give a party to which he invites the evangelist and his former cronies. Every man who experiences conversion must find a pattern of work and testimony that is valid for him. Life is too large and complex to permit even the pious to fashion a pattern of action that is appropriate for every man attracted to the Saviour.

*And the whole multitude sought to touch him: for there went virtue out of him, and healed them all (Luke 6:19).*

Great is the ministry of the touch! Men find real satisfaction in shaking hands with a notable; "Shake the hand that shook the hand of John L. Sullivan!" Religious bodies can profit from fostering a climate in which persons actually touch one another in order to heal wounds left from old quarrels. Individuals can begin to transform an enemy into a friend by a handshake that is given with pure motives. Physical encounter with the symbols which point to the Saviour (bread and wine of the communion feast) provide a touch-avenue fully as real as the touching of Jesus of Nazareth by His contemporaries.

*Blessed are ye, when men . . . shall separate you from their company . . . (Luke 6:22).*

Have you ever been omitted from a group or event because of a Christian conviction? Left out of a party because neighbors know you don't drink?

Here is something of a measuring rod. If you are always included, perhaps you'd better check yourself. Blessed is the power of nonadjustment. An out-of-step individualist whom "good fellows" regard as the sore thumb of the community may serve to call attention to a festering wound.

*And they that were sent, returning to the house, found the servant whole that had been sick (Luke 7:10).*

In its primary message, this miracle is not unique. It belongs in the class of all those whose message is, "Jesus is wholly God, subject to no limitations whatever."

But there is another facet of this story. Jesus heals the sick body of the slave at the request of his master. There is no move

79

to stir up political and economic changes by which the slave will gain his liberty and the institution of slavery will be abolished. That became a valid and legitimate concern of Christianity after many centuries had passed. But it is a gross error to make this or any other "reform" within the structure of time and space the crux of Christianity.

We cannot ignore the social gospel without distorting the compassion of Christ. But we can so elevate it to central position that we are concerned with making human corrections of human evils, rather than accepting divine remedies for problems that are insoluble in man's strength alone.

*And when the Lord saw her, he had compassion on her ... (Luke 7:13).*

Accompanied by a horde of eager curious and a small band of intimate seekers, the Master happened to meet a funeral procession. There is no indication that the forlorn widow whose son was on the bier made any outcry or entreaty directed toward Jesus. His response to her sorrow was spontaneous and unsolicited.

Many miracles stem from entreaty and urgent seeking. But some come without our asking. Great and wonderfully strange things are given us though we lack the wisdom to request them. Even in our most inspired prayers, we do not ask God for the fundamental processes of biology and chemistry that, somehow, are essential to the mysterious process we call "life."

*... the blind see, the lame walk, the lepers are cleansed, the deaf hear, the dead are raised, to the poor the gospel is preached (Luke 7:22)*

What a suggestive list! All the things enumerated fall into the category of strange and incredible works. There is no suggestion that one is a more profound marvel than another. Raising of the dead is on a par with causing the deaf to hear.

And the preaching of the gospel to the poor is a miracle of the same order. How much easier and more comfortable it is to preach the gospel to the rich, to the well-washed instead of the leprous, to clean-cut folk who hold their heads high instead of to those who limp lamely because their backs have been bent by social maladies. In those rare instances when men succeed in preaching the gospel to the poor, a divine miracle takes place.

*Now when the Pharisee which had bidden him saw it, he spake within himself, saying, This man, if he were a prophet, would have known who and what manner of woman this is that toucheth him (Luke 7:39).*

Habitually, we test in this fashion in order to decide whether or not a person is a prophet or an imposter, wise or ignorant. But the Pharisee made a major error. He presumed that Jesus did not share his own knowledge of fact, on the basis of his conclusion that Jesus did not act as he himself would have acted.

Actually, Jesus was fully aware that the woman was a sinner. But from that knowledge He drew conclusions different from those of the Pharisee, and so acted in a way that the Pharisee considered a proof of ignorance. Judging the guest by his own standards, the Pharisee could reach only one conclusion: this fellow is an imposter, not a prophet. This dramatic incident shows that we actually judge ourselves when we pass judgment on another's goodness or lack of it, or education, artistic merit, musical skill—or what have you.

*. . . Unto you it is given to know the mysteries of the kingdom of God: but to others in parables . . . (Luke 8:10).*

Reference to secrets and mysteries is too persistent to be ignored. What can be the meaning of this emphasis? Perhaps that Kingdom things are actually hidden. In order to find them, men must search. There can be no passive waiting, like little birds with their mouths open. Rather, there must be active, zealous effort on the part of one who would find new depth of understanding.

*Take heed therefore how ye hear: for whosoever hath, to him shall be given; and whosoever hath not, from him shall be taken even that which he seemeth to have (Luke 8:18).*

This feedback effect operates in every area where men search for understanding. Lifelong study of music brings new meaning from every fresh hearing of an opera that the beginner will, at the first hearing, reject as meaningless. A bird watcher hears notes that the amateur does not catch. The reader of Scripture who skims along in perfunctory fashion because it is strange to him will miss much that has great impact upon the mind of a saint; each fresh reading will reveal new and deeper meanings.

To the beginner, this phenomenon says: take courage, do not despair, work hard, and be patient in the knowledge that no harvest is immediate. To the veteran seeker, it says: continue growing, be unwilling to rest at the highest point already achieved, use your skill and experience to help you find something better.

*. . . My mother and my brethren are these which hear the word of God, and do it (Luke 8:21).*

Above, in the parable of the soils, Jesus has already shown that a verbal presentation of truth serves as a balance to weigh souls of those who listen. Here the idea is repeated and reinforced. Incredibly, capacity to listen (partly a gift of God, partly shaped by the individual in his use of his freedom) is a standard of kinship. It is more real and important than are biological ties!

That is hard for us to swallow; we balk at the idea. One of the reasons is that it is much easier for us to measure blood relationship than bonds of sympathetic understanding. We couldn't operate a society in which "kinship" would be traced in terms of sympathy for ideas—though that is necessarily a factor in the welding of individuals into nations. God's ways of determining which persons belong to the household of faith are too complex for us to manipulate. At best, we can make a stumbling approximation by extending the concept of "Christian brotherhood" past boundaries of race, economics, and national allegiance.

*. . . he went up into the ship, and returned . . . (Luke 8:37).*
Jesus does not violate personality. He knocks on the door of the human heart; but when a householder orders Him off the premises, He will return to another place of work. Cultures and individuals can effectively succeed in getting the Master to leave them in their isolation.

*And Herod said, John have I beheaded: but who is this, of whom I hear such things? . . . (Luke 9:9).*
Evil men think they win permanent victories by slaying prophets. They are under the delusion that there can be finality through violence, so are perplexed when another divine messenger appears to trouble and accuse them.

*. . . If any man will come after me, let him deny himself, and take up his cross daily, and follow me (Luke 9:23).*
Emphasis upon a "daily" pattern of life is central in the gospel message. One-day-a-week seeking for God limps and hops. Lacking some daily discipline, there is no keeping close behind Jesus. Even in cross-bearing that stems from cheerful surrender of life, there can be no once-for-all leap into dedicated service. Rather, there is a new cross to be lifted each day. At any time, the day's burden may be so fearful that it is repudiated. Those who are spiritually callous do not see the problem, for they have assumed so light and comfortable a cross that it does not rub the shoulders.

*. . . they kept it close, and told no man in those days any of those things which they had seen (Luke 9:36).*
A really stupendous event may have either of two effects: it

may set one to babbling without restraint; or it may seal one's lips. Perhaps the latter is the more profound result. It points to an experience so powerful that the recipient feels he cannot communicate it to another. There is no common ground for discussion with one who lacks an equivalent experience. That is the root of many problems of communication among those who are alike in seeking God, but who differ in the pattern of their religious experience.

*And as he was yet a-coming, the devil threw him down . . . (Luke 9:42).*

Satan is a doughty fighter. Even when one is actually en route to the altar—going to Jesus—the evil one within continues to struggle. Short of the unity that comes of yielding, short of absolute victory (however temporary), there is no relief.

*But they understood not this saying, and it was hid from them . . . (Luke 9:45).*

Too much, we have discounted the strangeness of the gospel. Over and over, it offends or puzzles even those closest to Jesus. There is no insuperable problem involved in lack of understanding when it is frankly recognized. In such an instance it may be an asset in the search for faith, for it may function as a path of wonder. But there are major problems when one hurriedly leaps to the affirmation "I do understand," when his understanding is actually superficial and limited. Perhaps we need to examine our religious views carefully; if we find no major puzzles, that may tell us that our eyes are dull. (See 10:22; 18:34.)

*And when his disciples James and John saw this, they said, Lord, wilt thou that we command fire to come down from heaven, and consume them . . . ? (Luke 9:54).*

This is the typical attitude of the zealous religionist. Religion raises barriers as well as lowers them. In a famous wartime prayer,

Billy Sunday's fervent invocation of God's fury upon the Huns caused the U. S. Congress to break into applause. Let us watch ourselves when we begin to find ourselves so righteously indignant that we consider asking Jehovah to blast men down. For though we accompany Jesus, that attitude is sure to bring a rebuke from Him.

*. . . The harvest truly is great, but the labourers are few: pray ye therefore the Lord of the harvest, that he would send forth labourers . . . (Luke 10:2).*

A major principle of leadership is involved. Jesus states a problem: a great harvest is ready to be gathered, but workers are too few. Then He draws a conclusion: pray for more workers.

Today, we are more likely to suggest a different course of action: redouble your efforts, work with frantic zeal, knock yourself out for the cause.

There is a great difference between merely working hard and working for the right goals. A leader who is effective may devote his time to recruiting ten helpers—instead of trying to do the work of ten men.

*Which now of these three, thinkest thou, was neighbour unto him that fell among the thieves? (Luke 10:36).*

Has modern Christendom unconsciously fostered a major distortion here?

We prize this story; make much of it; tell it with approval. But we call it "The Parable of the Good Samaritan" rather than "The Parable of the Neighbors." Use of the former title may still imply, in a most Satanic and subtle fasion, that it is actually atypical for any Samaritan of any culture to be good. Though in this instance he is good, that is so unusual that the hero of the story must have a special distinguishing label which sets him apart from run-of-the-mill Samaritans.

Use of a title that would emphasize the problem of "neighbor" would take the focus from racial and religious differences that mark the Samaritan. Such an emphasis would cause the parable to center upon the question of what constitutes a "neighbor"— that person whom the law of God requires us to love as fully and unswervingly as we love ourselves. For the message of the parable is not so much that we should exult over the fact that sometimes a member of a despised race conducts himself in more Christian manner than a Methodist preacher. The real weight of the parable goes back to verse 27; and the story itself is intended to open up the "neighbor concept" and show that it must be applied to all men, including those Samaritans who would come along and strip the wounded man of anything left behind by those earlier neighbors, the robbers.

An impossible demand? Of course! That is the heart of 10:27; it requires man to do that which his nature makes him incapable of doing by dint of mere striving.

*Consider the ravens: for they neither sow nor reap; which neither have storehouse nor barn; and God feedeth them . . . (Luke 12:24).*

There is a point of view from which this may be challenged and judged to offer poor comfort: "God's feeding is rather uncertain; almost any day, one can walk out and find a dead bird who may have starved because he had no storehouse. Can't we have a more powerful guarantee than this?"

No, for human life, with all man's striving added to the care of God, is also uncertain. There is only one certainty in it: it will come to an end. Its total duration will be an instant so brief that it has no significance in terms of time. If man's life is to be meaningful, it must derive that meaning from some other dimension. For even if a man should by care succeed in living 150 years, that is nothing against even one short glacial epoch.

Yet a man who lives effectively for thirty years may have made a contribution. Forget the "length" criterion. Trust God to maintain those background conditions that are essential to preservation of any form of life. Thrust out boldly, living each day as though it might, in God's providence, be the last. If it should actually prove to be the last, that is incidental in the light of the cosmic question: how has your life (long or short) been spent?

*. . . it cannot be that a prophet perish out of Jerusalem (Luke 13:33).*

In its basic and literal sense, this is of course intimately related to the long stream of Jewish prophecy.

There is a secondary interpretation, however. For the verdict suggests that, literally, every genuine prophet, whose message is so fresh and profound that it shakes society to the point that men turn on the disturber to slay him, is a prophet who can perish only in some "Jerusalem." There is no magic involved, nor is this prophecy in the sense of prediction. Rather, it is the inevitable result of spiritual laws: for at whatever place an authentic prophet may perish, there men will later gather to erect markers and establish a new Jerusalem—a shrine where men of later epochs will come to turn their eyes back to the great figure of the past who perished here.

*And it came to pass, as he went into the house of one of the chief Pharisees to eat bread on the sabbath day, that they watched him (Luke 14:1).*

Problem: why did Jesus eat with Pharisees so frequently? (See 11:37.) Does this practice indicate unwillingness to give up any group as hopeless—in spite of criticism and hostility? When should one stop fraternizing with opponents? How does one go about finding the moral courage to seek converts even in situations deliberately set up for the purpose of testing and accusing?

Notice, too, how feasts were occasions for teaching, in this chapter, addressed to both guests and hosts. This suggests that valid religion is too vital to be compartmentalized and set apart into a conventional pattern. There was no occasion whatever that could not provide an opportunity for teaching. Hence it was as natural to dine with Pharisees as to read in the synagogue.

*And he put forth a parable to those which were bidden, when he marked how they chose out the chief rooms . . . (Luke 14:7).*

Even the best are "human" in little things. An old saint will choose the cushioned pew, glare at a visitor who accidentally takes her place. At pastors' school, men of God will jostle one another in order to get into the front of the chow line. In some respects, it is easier to be a martyr than to master selfish tendencies in the trivial things of life.

*For I say unto you, That none of those men which were bidden shall taste of my supper (Luke 14:24).*

It is right and proper to emphasize the gospel of the second chance. At the same time, we must recognize that there may be an element of finality in any particular instance of refusal. We do not know which of our decisions will have such finality; life is too uncertain to know that in advance. But in every life, there come times when a "no" to God cannot be altered or recalled.

*. . . the children of this world are in their generation wiser than the children of light (Luke 16:8).*

Men with false and limited goals are often more zealous in pursuing them than are men with true and high goals. Jesus enjoins "simplicity of mind" and childlikeness, but never gives His blessing to spiritual inertia or intellectual laziness. Though the church must never fall into the trap of establishing for itself the goals of the world, it must be as zealous as the world in pursuing its own ends.

88

Perhaps this applies to those who smugly assert that all one needs to do is to "accept Jesus Christ and be saved," without making the intellectual and spiritual adventure that is required in order to explore the meaning of the Saviour and of the redemption He offers. For this much seems evident—though the sons of the world pursue false values, they know exactly what they seek and go after it with fervor; sons of light are too often content with fuzzy goals and inherited enthusiasm.

*He that is faithful in that which is least is faithful also in much . . . (Luke 16:10).*

Everybody has opportunity and capacity for faithfulness in what we call "little things." This provides a training ground for character. Attitudes and values built up in dealing with little things will transfer over into the realm of big things.

Fretting impatiently and hoping for a chance to "do something big" is not only wasteful; it is defeating. Only the man who has already won muscles through mastery of little things will be strong enough to handle big things when they are encountered. Hence there is a democracy here: no man is excluded from the fellowship of mastering little things, if he will but accept the challenge.

*. . . when ye shall have done all those things which are commanded you, say, We are unprofitable servants . . . (Luke 17:10).*

Be eternally vigilant against the deadly serpent, pride. Even in the moment of highest victory, remember that you are a creature. Never forget your limitedness, your incapacity to win that perfection which alone satisfies God. For there is no method whatever by which a man can accomplish results that afford a valid ground for pride in what he has done. Always, success in the spiritual quest seems real only when measured by lesser men; when God's standards are applied, every man is a failure.

*. . . There was in a city a judge, which feared not God, neither regarded man (Luke 18:2).*

Perhaps the combination of attitudes is much more than accidental. Any man who does not fear God is unlikely to have effective respect for men. This has much to say about our public officials, the whole problem of "democracy on trial." It is also a hint that there is no permanent solution for the problem of "poor officials." No matter what the form of government, some men will come to power in spite of the fact that they do not merit a high place. Every attempt to solve human problems by changing the form of government or by getting "better" leaders is doomed to failure. There is no method whatever by which we can approach a lasting Utopia. We must look beyond political reforms, however important and helpful they may be, to the Kingdom that is not on earth.

*For the Son of man is come to seek and to save that which was lost (Luke 19:10).*

This is a promise of unbounded forgiveness, the kind that even takes in tax collectors (at whom we in the pulpit are likely to take sly digs, indicating that according to our sense of values, the tax collector can get from us something valuable and important).

But it is more than a promise of forgiveness. It also points to a prerequisite for salvation. In the case of inanimate things, lostness is an impersonal condition; but in the case of men it is very personal. No man can be found until he clearly and definitely knows that he is lost. So long as he regards himself as neatly established on the shelf (whatever the nature of his shelf of values and ideals) there is no possibility of radical conversion and salvation. Zacchaeus differed from masses of others in his consciousness of needing to be found.

*And take heed to yourselves, lest at any time your hearts be
overcharged with surfeiting, and drunkenness, and cares of this
life . . . (Luke 21:34).*

Here is a strange trio! Viewed from a particular set of values,
dissipation and drunkenness are much worse than mere worry.
But from another viewpoint, fretting is as damaging as tippling—
for both inhibit sensitivity. By taking command of the mind,
petty worries make "watchfulness" impossible; one cannot both
worry and watch at the same time.

*And truly the Son of man goeth, as it was determined: but woe
unto that man by whom he is betrayed! (Luke 22:22).*

We seldom recognize the full depths of woe in which the be-
trayer was involved. For in fact, the betrayal of Judas was
wholly unsuccessful. His one role was to point out—or identify
—Jesus. This was a very small undertaking, for Jesus was a
public figure. When Jesus went on trial, Judas was not there to
testify against Him. So far as the effect of the work of Judas
was concerned, the betrayal was futile. He did not succeed in
bringing his Master to the point of conviction. So, in a sense,
the only element of success in his betrayal was linked with his
betrayal of himself.

That can be taken as the type of all spiritual betrayals—the
person who sells his convictions is the only one who really suf-
fers as a result of his actions. Others who are his victims may
suffer in a physical sense; but that is brief, and without cosmic
significance.

*Then said he unto them, But now, he that hath a purse, let him
take it . . . (Luke 22:36).*

This set of instructions is quite different from that issued
earlier. Changing conditions require changed techniques and
varied emphases. It is false and stupid to think that one approach

to Christian witnessing must be used universally because it has been successful under some circumstances. Good apostles will vary their plan of procedure to fit the needs of the hour.

*And Peter went out, and wept bitterly (Luke 22:62).*

Everything in this dramatic story points to the conclusion that it could have come to St. Luke from only one source—Peter himself. Had he not told of the series of incidents, there would have been no way to learn that they took place. This points to an important facet of the personality of this many-sided man. He did not hide the uncomplimentary truth about himself. Perhaps the very willingness to confess his own failure, after having wept over it, helped him to become the key figure in the infant church which was so soon to be born.

*And they were the more fierce, saying, He stirreth up the people . . . (Luke 23:5).*

Remember that it is a group of important religious leaders who are pressing the charge. Perhaps there is nothing that is more likely to offend the top dignitaries of most religious systems than acts which lead to "stirring up the people." Official religion seldom wants the people aroused.

*And their words seemed to them as idle tales, and they believed them not (Luke 24:11).*

It is not strange that the resurrection should be a major stumbling block in the thought of many moderns. We make a mistake to think it was easy and natural to the "credulous" disciples of the first century. They had to struggle with the idea, too. Even after having accompanied Jesus and listened to His teaching, they were totally unprepared for this incredible event. Every attempt to make it credible and logical is a distortion. We must recognize it for what it is: a difficult mystery. All of

Chapter 24 is a document attesting bewilderment, doubt, and confusion—on the part of those who were in the best position to comprehend.

*. . . they yet believed not for joy . . . (Luke 24:41).*

There are things so good they are incredible—to be accepted only after doubt, hesitation, and inquiry. That is the case with many deep truths of the gospel. Some of the promises are so life-transforming that they are extremely hard to accept.

*. . . tarry ye in the city of Jerusalem, until ye be endued with power from on high (Luke 24:49).*

There are times when the most fruitful of all activities is to do nothing. Such waiting is not passive, however; it is charged with dynamic, for it includes expectant anticipation. That can bring the power essential for a great task. Rushing out too hurriedly, not willing to wait for power, can lead to disaster.

# THE GOSPEL OF
# John

*All things were made by him; and without him was not any thing
made that was made (John 1:3).*

Despite all our attention concentrated upon aspects of the
industrial age, man actually is not a maker of material things in
the fundamental sense. He is adept in working transformation and
in modifying the basic materials given him. But man makes nothing that is a "raw stuff." God made and shaped the background,
and furnished all the ingredients that man mixes in new pro-
portions and shapes in order to do what we call "making things."

Once this basic matter is forgotten or obscured, man the
creature loses sight of his limitations and lack of self-sufficiency.
Proud in his power as the only creative species on earth, measuring himself by nonhuman species of today and primitive men
of yesterday, modern man becomes the most glorious figure in
his field of vision. It is only when he sees himself against the
transforming might of God the Maker that man the shaper sees
himself in true perspective.

*And the light shineth in darkness; and the darkness compre-
hended it not (John 1:5).*

Given a candlelit room, it is possible to focus on either
of two valid sets of meanings. One may emphasize how much
darkness and how little light there is—or one may marvel at the
wonderful reality that light is not overcome. Here, as in many
areas, it is an error to make too much of quantity. One may
survey the quantity of human depravity and become cynical,
pessimistic. Or one may dwell on the wholly stupendous fact
that some men live in such a way that God's light shines through
them. This can become the focal point of meaning, giving significance to everything seen in relation to the central idea. Here
it is the plus rather than the minus that must be seen and magnified.

*No man hath seen God at any time . . . (John 1:18).*

The enormous depth of this statement often escapes us. There
is no bridge between God and man. Even the revelation in Christ
is a declaration—the highest possible, but not a full means of
"seeing" God the Father in His entirety. Perhaps the greatest
modern heresy is that of believing we completely comprehend
God, even to the extent of competing with Him.

*Then said they unto him, Who art thou? that we may give an
answer to them that sent us . . . (John 1:22).*

This is a very poor motive for wanting information. It is an
example of action directed toward a secondary goal. Priests and
Levites were not open to personal transformation; they were
simply serving as channels to transmit a message in which they
had no vital personal interest.

Teaching can be like that: "A college lecture is a process by
which words are transferred from the notes of the instructor to
the notes of the student without passing through the mind of
either." Much that parades as teaching in the Sunday school is

96

wholly devoid of life, for the teacher is concerned only to please those who sent him. Communication that matters is firsthand and vital.

*And I saw, and bare record that this is the Son of God (John 1:34).*

There is no substitute for the impelling power of seeing through personal encounter. Acceptance of secondhand reports is stultifying; a continuous search for firsthand experience is the heart of the religious life.

Encounter leads to witness. Note that one does not have to be able to give a logical explanation of his experience in order to witness to it; it is possible to declare that Shrimp Arnaud is good, without being able to explain why it is good. There is no role more magnificent than that of the witness who bears record to glorious experiences.

*The day following Jesus would go forth into Galilee, and findeth Philip . . . (John 1:43).*

This is the city in which Andrew has already found Cephas. But it is the Master himself, independent of the new disciple, who finds Philip.

Jesus can be presented to men by and through men who are His disciples. But He is not confined to working through professed followers. He makes direct overtures as well. So the witness should remain humble, never daring to think of himself as an exclusive channel through which the Saviour may go to men, and refraining from counting "his" converts because he is humbly aware that Jesus may have made direct contact with the latest convert in one's own city.

*. . . thou shalt see greater things than these (John 1:50).*

Ability to see a marvel in a simple event is not a terminus to knowing, but a point of departure. It is a promise of much greater

97

things to come. Any person who must begin with great things—heaven opened and angels passing back and forth—succeeds only in closing doors. He inhibits the very revelation that he seeks, for until he has found capacity to see God in commonplace things he lacks capacity to see Him in the most stupendous kinds of revelation.

*And the third day there was a marriage . . . (John 2:1).*
Surely it was not accidental that a wedding feast should be the occasion for a dramatic lesson. For in John's thought, it is the function of the Saviour to make possible a wedding between man and God. Through the spiritual union symbolized by the wine of Jesus' blood, that soul which becomes a bride of the Lamb finds things better than anything yet tasted—even on the joyful occasion of a bridal feast.

*. . . thou hast kept the good wine until now (John 2:10).*
This is the focal point of the story. Jesus was superior to the old prophets. Such a concept involves one's philosophy of history. It challenges all views by which the "good old days" are automatically contrasted with the degenerate present. It hints that though God acts consistently and lawfully, we do not fully understand His ways. We do wrong to prejudge the future on the basis of the past. God is capable of giving good new gifts that quite defy our attempts at either anticipation or explanation.

*. . . make not my Father's house an house of merchandise (John 2:16).*
At first look, this seems a much milder warning than that implied in the language, "den of thieves." But the difference may actually be superficial. Abuse of God's house is abuse, and the degree of wrong is not the central issue. However innocent, even worthy, the entrance of a commercial enterprise and the commercial motive into God's house is dangerous. For it pro-

vides an easy way in which a secondary goal may be pushed into such prominence that it obscures or dominates a primary goal. This is a major element in all money-raising for "good causes," all loyal work for an institution. It has suggestive implications concerning right and wrong motivation behind bazaars, rummage sales, and even barbecue suppers.

*But Jesus . . . knew all men, And needed not that any should testify of man: for he knew what was in man (John 2:24, 25).*

It is John who sings of the pre-existent Word of God—and John who emphasizes the real humanity of the Saviour. This tender allusion testifies to the reality of the incarnation. Christ can understand us because He is one of us. This is a major facet of Christian doctrine.

Yet it suggests a paradox. For it includes both utter pessimism about man and unbounded optimism. Jesus knows that the natural (self-centered) man is weak, proud, ready to send a Saviour to the cross. This is not simply true of an occasional bad man; it marks good men—pillars of the church and community. Yet it was precisely for such men that Jesus deliberately came, with premeditation giving Himself. Hence, His self-giving is a vote of confidence in the potential and the capacity-to-become of the redeemed man.

*. . . a man of the Pharisees, named Nicodemus . . . (John 3:1).*

It was this official opponent, interested enough in the radical message of Jesus to come by night, who evoked the overpowering interpretation of the new birth. Only a moment of severe challenge is likely to produce the most exalted interpretations of a teacher.

Though the context suggests that Nicodemus was not persuaded, this is not reported. For John's purpose, the question of whether or not a particular inquirer came to believe was not a matter of fundamental importance. He did not follow the practice of publishing lists of prominent converts in order to attract hordes of lesser men. For John, the majority of converts remain uncounted and anonymous.

*. . . thou art a teacher come from God . . . (John 3:2).*
This is close to the peak of humanistic appreciation of Jesus. It involves belief in God the Creator, as well as in man's capacity to know Him at some level. It includes a profound recognition of Jesus' originality and depth as a teacher. But this is not Christianity.

John's account hints that Nicodemus failed in his quest, by remaining on the level at which Jesus is seen as a good man, perhaps the best of all men, but still merely a man. Perhaps it is not accidental that Nicodemus represents the cultured, educated, upright group in the society of his day. Such men abound in every epoch, and it is precisely these—lacking the fervor and hunger of the masses, restrained by barriers of culture and knowledge—who tend to become the Unitarians of their period.

*The wind bloweth where it listeth, and thou hearest the sound thereof, but canst not tell whence it cometh, and whither it goeth: so is every one that is born of the Spirit (John 3:8).*
Though we must necessarily make wide use of logic and of factual knowledge, let us not fall into the trap of assuming that with these tools we can resolve all mysteries. Far from it. Beyond all that we know, and not necessarily in direct continuity with it, there is an area of the unknown. We can accept it without pretending to be able to explain it. Indeed, there is no other way in which its existence can be recognized effectively. So long as we insist upon having neat explanations for all that is, we shall end by treating the inexplicable as nonexistent.

Deep things of the spirit are not to be reduced to equations. When we try to perform such an operation and seem to achieve a degree of success, we have done nothing more than discover a technique that works under some circumstances—but we still may not know why it works or what its ultimate meaning may be. By calling on men to recognize the area of the wonderful, then consciously to apply its possibilities to their lives, Jesus opens big doors for growth and discovery and revelation.

*And as Moses lifted up the serpent in the wilderness, even so must the Son of man be lifted up (John 3:14).*
Much of our imagery is linked with the general idea that success consists in mounting upward or being elevated. Jesus takes the same metaphor and adopts it by deliberately inverting it. His uplifting is to be complete degradation and shame; paradoxically, that is the avenue to absolute glory. Any uplifting that is sought in the conventional sense, for its own sake and not as a way of self-giving, may dim one's vision and cause him to lose sight of his real goal.

*. . . A man can receive nothing, except it be given him from heaven (John 3:27).*
Modern emphasis is upon man's striving, his seizure of knowledge and power. Here is an opposite emphasis. Unless man has been given certain basic capacities that do not result from his own striving, he is literally incapable of achievement. He is a creator, but also a creature whose creative capacity is as truly given as won, as really conferred as attained.

*. . . he that is of the earth is earthly . . . (John 3:31).*
Man is earth-bound. He cannot transcend limitations of his creaturehood. Perhaps the chief lesson man needs to learn is centered here. For this is the antithesis of "Progress is our most important product," an advertising slogan that reflects unbounded optimism about man's capacities to rise above the limitations of manhood.

*. . . Jacob's well was there . . . (John 4:6).*

Here is a land steeped in time. At every hand, there are tangible mementos of the past. Modern preoccupation with "progress," in the sense that thought is largely oriented forward, was all but wholly absent from first-century Palestine. Instead, there was a focus upon the past, whose glories were such that the present seemed dim by comparison.

Such a point of view is difficult if not impossible to capture in a land where tangible evidences of the distant past are non-existent. Roots of contemporary western culture are shallow in this respect. We not only feel that a building erected in the last century is old; we are likely to regard it as an anachronism by virtue of no other quality than its age.

We desperately need some deeper and stronger roots that go back to the wells of the past. In this respect, the move toward adoption of what is in some respects a good thing, such as the Revised Standard Version of Scripture, has disvalues that may actually outweigh positive values. Far more than a young and contemporary book, we need a Book that speaks to us out of the past in order to remind us that the present is neither definitive nor permanent.

*. . . the Jews have no dealings with the Samaritans (John 4:9).*

Wherever two or more distinct groups of persons come into contact, tension is inevitable. Differences may be cultural, religious, racial, economic, or political. Possibility of anything approaching a permanent solution is doubtful, for the nature of man is involved here.

Notice, however, that while tension may be inevitable, the forms that grow up under it are local and transient. Ways in which Jesus' contemporaries refused dealings with Samaritans were not identical with mores that are established in other times and places. Divisive customs are local, rather than sacred; they are limited, rather than universal.

*The woman saith unto him, Sir, I perceive that thou art a prophet (John 4:19).*

It would have been easy for the accused woman to reach quite different conclusions: to lash out against the stranger as a spy or an agent of the enemy or simply a meddler in the affairs of others. Here is a specific example of the way in which one's personal judgments also judge her. For her conclusion reflects some basic attitudes from which the woman surveyed Jesus and His sayings.

Regardless of how one may define a prophet (and the woman's view seems quite low), recognition is not necessarily automatic. It may take a considerable degree of acquaintance with a person in order to come to regard him as quite different from what he seemed earlier. Even after such a change has taken place, there are wide variations in ability to understand the message of a true prophet.

Perhaps we can't restrain ourselves from leaping to judgments about the persons we meet: our friends and neighbors, members of the family, a new colleague. We quickly conclude that one is a dumb fool, another a conceited ass, still another a lazy glutton. But in reaching such judgments—which we can't fully avoid doing—we lay ourselves open. For the real inadequacies may lie in our own inability to appreciate qualities of the one whom we label.

*. . . when he is come, he will tell us all things (John 4:25).*

This is a terrible, but a perennial, fallacy. Men expect through some cosmic event to gain a divine revelation that will banish all questions. But the nature of communication is such that even God does not pour into any mind more meaning than that mind is capable of receiving and using. God's power to reveal is limited and conditioned by man's capacity to receive—human blindness, self-centeredness, and ignorance. That this is the heart of the passage is clearly indicated by the next sentence. This woman who

103

is so ecstatic in hoping for a divine revelation has actually been in face-to-face encounter with the Word made flesh, but doesn't know it, and is unable to appropriate the full message He offers. There has been encounter, but only limited communication.

No matter how ardently He may be expected, even Messiah does not violate personality and make people see Him as He is; men may argue with Him and not know it. Hence, to them, He is not Messiah. A shallow and excuse-based hope such as that of the text is utterly vain.

*. . . Except ye see signs and wonders, ye will not believe (John 4:48).*

The paradox of this dilemma is that the person who places greatest premiums on signs and marvels is least capable of seeing valid ones. The demand for wonders constitutes its own negation. Conversely, one who no longer needs signs in order to believe in God's greatness has gained capacity to find marvels in every event.

What is the remedy? Steady searching even in complete darkness, pressing on with no certainty of arriving, searching for light so earnestly that one gains capacity to use what little light he has as a path along which to proceed into radiance.

*. . . there was a feast of the Jews; and Jesus went up to Jerusalem (John 5:1).*

Jesus did not spurn the holy feast—but went! He used all human occasions to implement His mission and message. He did not withdraw and hold up His garments to avoid pollution. That is, He was not too holy to participate in an observance that was less than the best.

*In these lay a great multitude of impotent folk, of blind, halt, withered, waiting for the moving of the water (John 5:3).*

Waiting in the porches. . . .

Passive, faithfully and eagerly holding out their hands for God to pour rice into their cups.

This attitude is often, if not usually, a last resort. It is to be adopted when medicine has proved impotent.

But healing followed a valid personal encounter with Jesus, in the absence of the customary signs! Glory! When Jesus is really met, all the conventional techniques fade into insignificance!

*. . . whosoever then first after the troubling of the water stepped in was made whole of whatsoever disease he had (John 5:4).*

There are some genuine cure-alls. But they are few and far between. Only a fraction of the frantic, patient seekers find what they are hunting.

Cures at the pool of Bethesda are examples of special instances of divine power, but are typical of most manifestations in the ratio of cures. Many seek; few find. Only really desperate men even try. So desperation may be the real avenue to healing.

*. . . Wilt thou be made whole? (John 5:6).*

Here, "whole" is more suggestive than the "healed" of the Revised Standard Version. For wholeness is a total goal, dynamic, never fully achieved. It involves the question of self-realization in all areas: physical, mental, and spiritual. A self less than whole is unfulfilled, lopsided, empty.

Burning, possessive desire for wholeness in this absolute sense is a magic key to many a cure. Even physical healings are likely, as in this case, to include mental and spiritual factors.

*Jesus saith unto him, Rise, take up thy bed, and walk (John 5:8).*

Here, the sick man was waiting for someone to perform a service for him in order to give him an advantage over other seekers.

But his vital encounter with Jesus has as its cutting edge the fact that he didn't actually need what he had waited all those years hoping to get. Instead of having to rush into the troubled waters, all he needed (in the light of a divine encounter) was to get up and do for himself some of the things he had depended on others to do for him.

There is an individualism that is dangerous because it includes too little recognition of man's dependence upon others. But there is a socialism that is equally dangerous, because it includes so great a dependence upon others that individual initiative is stifled. In every age, multitudes are prone to lie infirm because they fall into one or the other of these traps.

*And immediately the man was made whole, and took up his bed, and walked: and on the same day was the sabbath (John 5:9).*

John's story comes to a dramatic climax. This vital matter was not previously hinted, but reserved until the reader has questioned, wondered, and marveled at the healing. Then the sudden introduction of a new element, the matter of the Sabbath, takes the reader by surprise. It leads to quick reaction: indignation at the Pharisees. In all operations, it is in the most holy moments, most hallowed situations, that the very pious protest any violation of the code that will result in so unrestrained an act as a miracle of healing.

*The Jews therefore said unto him that was cured, It is the sabbath day: it is not lawful for thee to carry thy bed (John 5:10).*

By nature, authority must always resent and try to curb miracle. For miracle is antithetical to the authoritarian position itself. Miracle challenges security and order, makes the established uncertain, topples the status quo, explodes neat systems, demands changes in the certainty with which convictions are held. This element of creativity is constantly making war upon man's desire to find comfort in the rigidity of his systems.

*And he that was healed wist not who it was . . . (John 5:13).*

Where there is desperate, long-continued need, it is not always best to demand credentials of one who offers help. Indeed, perhaps

106

a man is not really ready to be healed so long as he interrogates the one who offers him a helping hand. Without the faith that is a rebound from sheer desperation and bottomless despair, men may find it difficult or impossible to accept divine aid. So long as one quizzes the witness sent by God, he is not likely to gain the message. He must be an actor rather than an analyst in order to seize the Word offered to him. That charlatans and fakers take advantage of this situation in no way reduces its significance.

*. . . The hour is coming, and now is, when the dead shall hear the voice of the Son of God: and they that hear shall live (John 5:25).*

For each individual, the crucial instant of history is that in which he is confronted with the Word of God. God speaks through all events, but most clearly through the living Word—the Son.

Those who are dead are not necessarily laid out in tombs and wrapped in winding sheets. Many men build sepulchers of pride, lust, or laziness and live in them for years before life departs from the body. One who is in such a state of living death may gain freedom by listening to the message of Jesus. Effective hearing leads to opening of the tomb; there is a passing into a new dimension as far removed from the old as is physical life from physical death. Those who choose not to hear will be condemned to remain in the old, lower state—blind even to the existence of that which they have rejected.

*Search the scriptures, for in them ye think ye have eternal life: and they are they which testify of me. And ye will not come to me, that ye might have life (John 5:39-40).*

Lacking vital contact with God's living Word—transmitted most powerfully though not exclusively through the Saviour—written records of revelation become academic, legalistic, closed rather than open, restrictive rather than redemptive. Though such written messages do bear witness to the Saviour who is life, they do not so fully contain Him that all readers automatically seize truth. Only those who turn to Scripture in the light of contact with the living Word will in the pages of the Book find full life.

*How can ye believe, which receive honour one of another, and seek not the honour that cometh from God only? (John 5:44).*

By seeking honor on one's own level—that is, the material, physical and human plane—one inhibits the search for a wholly different kind of honor that can come from God alone. Full of complacency at the secondary and derived kind of honor that is won from other men, one lacks both motive and sensitivity for participating in the true search. This makes it difficult or impossible to respond even to the supreme instance of divine revelation: Jesus Himself.

*When Jesus therefore perceived that they would come and take him by force, to make him a king, he departed again into a mountain himself alone (John 6:15).*

Men demand the luxury of subjecting themselves to authority. When a mighty leader does not seek material power, crowds eagerly try to force it upon him. For there is no state more comfortable than that of subjection and dependence; difficult choices are eliminated, for when questions arise they may be referred to the king. In a democracy, men who think they hate all kings are quick to elevate entertainers and celebrities to the status of popular idols who serve as arbiters of taste and conduct.

Jesus departed because He felt that to be threatened with elevation to a throne is about the most frightening prospect that can be faced. It is time to flee when crowds offer a crown!

*. . . they willingly received him into the ship: and immediately the ship was at the land whither they went (John 6:21).*

This is an allegory of the voyage of life. Men who take the

ship of devotion are headed for a specific destination—the Kingdom. But they make slow progress in their search for it; they row
mightily, but travel only five and twenty or thirty furlongs.

When Jesus is taken aboard, the ship of life immediately reaches
its destination—here and now. There is a victory that transcends
the limits of time with its past, present, and future. This miracle
that we call "salvation" because we must give it a name in order
to discuss it, is quite beyond logical analysis. To dissect it is to
destroy it. We can only accept it in faith—and be transported to
the harbor that is sought.

*. . . What shall we do, that we might work the works of God?*
*(John 6:28).*

This is a perennial question, both within and without Christianity. In every epoch, in some fashion, men have longed to do
the works of God—no matter how dimly or uncertainly they
have seen God. It is a trait deep in man to want to work God's
works. But men in their blindness do not know how; they want
directions, guides, and highways.

Jesus sums up the matter in one sentence (verse 29): "This is
the work of God, that ye believe on him whom he hath sent."

Belief always issues in action of some kind, of course. But belief
does not necessarily grow out of action in the same fashion. We
often spend our lives frantically trying to do mighty works: build
buildings, enlist members, find supporters, convince doubters—
when all the time we are neglecting the really basic task of searching for a deeper and more vital kind of belief out of which material
works that matter will come as by-products. Such achievements
will seldom be identical with the "works" that are produced by
dedication to works alone.

*. . . This is the work of God, that ye believe on him whom he*
*hath sent (John 6:29).*

Men must work; there is no escaping the choice of a goal

(whether specified consciously or not), and choice of things that seem to lead toward that goal. But it is one thing to work for physical food and quite another to labor for food of the soul. Success in the latter enterprise centers in achieving vital belief. (See verse 28.)

In our modern culture, we find it very hard to accept Jesus' principle in anything other than an adulterated sense. There is no problem in conceiving of God's work as being performed through evangelistic calling or raising money for missions, or even box suppers at the church to foster good fellowship and growth of the congregation. But private, personal, immeasurable believing doesn't seem much like work for God.

Acceptance of Jesus' formula leaves us troubled. For there is the startling implication that any numbskull can measure the number of dollars he collects, while no one can measure the vitality of another's believing. We are left in a most uncomfortable position; we can't be precisely sure who is and who isn't working for God, and cannot measure the success of any witness.

Such a state of affairs is intolerable; we much prefer to define God's work in terms of things we can measure.

*. . . I am the bread of life: he that cometh to me shall never hunger; and he that believeth on me shall never thirst (John 6:35).*

Any real comprehension of the metaphors must rest upon the physical experience of hunger and of thirst. A typical American audience can't plumb the depths of the comparison as did Jesus' first-century hearers. Force of the imagery is dulled by the fact that few of us have been really hungry like the oppressed of Palestine, or thirsty like men who have travelled across semi-desert lands with a limited water supply.

Few religious experiments would be more dramatic, vivid, and meaningful than that of individual or group searching for the depth of this message—by deliberately becoming hungry and thirsty for God's sake, in order to experience the sharpness of longing so that the physical experience may be transferred to the religious realm and stimulate seekers to long for Christ as eagerly as for bread and water.

*The Jews then murmured at him, because he said, I am the bread which came down from heaven (John 6:41).*

Harmless and unexciting as this metaphor may sound to those whose ears are made dull by familiarity, it is actually explosive. Jesus' opponents recognized its dynamic. Instead of dismissing the Nazarene as a harmless enthusiast or a crackpot, they attacked Him as a dangerous radical, whose blasphemous words so outraged pious ears that He could not be suffered to live.

Note that the good folk of the day would not have insisted upon sending Jesus to the cross, had not they had their sense of propriety outraged. They feared the corruption of their children, and were distressed at possible results of a movement based on wholly outrageous claims.

Men of the present age are often repelled by the same illogical claim on the part of a man in history who announced himself to be God incarnate. Today, the typical denial takes the form of espousing some wholly logical and therefore comfortable brand of humanism.

*Many therefore of his disciples, when they had heard this, said, This is an hard saying; who can hear it? (John 6:60).*

The message of verses 43-63 is indeed hard to take!

Heard for the first time, with fresh ears, it seems brutal, insane, and wholly incredible. But, says Jesus, other teachings are simple and easy to understand by comparison with difficulties involved in grasping the meaning of the resurrection.

Notice that this strange message led to disaffection (verse 66). It still has that consequence. Men draw away from it, refuse to think of it, or devise nice formulas to explain away its difficulties.

We need to follow the opposite path, to focus on knotty problems and recognize that Christianity deliberately and gloriously rises above cozy explanations. It centers in divine mysteries. Lacking recognition of a more-than-human and supralogical element in the faith, men reduce it to a set of cultural goals and try to usher in heaven-on-earth.

*. . . How knoweth this man letters, having never learned? (John 7:15).*

Because Jesus was assumed to have had little or no formal schooling, it puzzled His opponents that He could read. Their question touches on a universal problem: the tendency of society to challenge a person who lacks the formal, conventional certification that is customarily associated with skill. No matter what one's degree of wisdom (which is beyond measurement), he may be attacked because he lacks some symbol of learning, which can be won by any dullard who plods his way through routine processes. This demand for credentials is a protective device which petty men keep ready at hand.

*He that speaketh of himself seeketh his own glory: but he that seeketh his glory that sent him, the same is true . . . (John 7:18).*

Conscious dedication to a goal outside the ego confers an authority that is beyond measurement, yet is real. This applies in salesmanship and in gospel singing, in journalism and in teaching a Sunday school class.

Such authority is not an automatic guarantee of "success." But it does give the witness a kind of "truth" that is highly significant. He is not preserved from making errors in points of fact—academic mistakes; but he is saved from the far more significant error of self-centeredness.

Nothing quite matches the power of a man who is not selling himself and his objectives, but is selling an idea to which he himself is captive. You may laugh at him, slash at him, and crucify him—but you cannot fail to hear him.

*. . . He that is without sin among you, let him first cast a stone
at her (John 8:7).*

Whether literal, as in the case of this wretched woman, or
figurative in quite different contexts, stoning is group action. It
seeks to do violence without individual responsibility; for it is
impossible to say what man's stone leads to death. In this respect
stoning is unlike hanging or shooting or stabbing; it is a nice, clean
way to kill—in such a fashion that no individual killer feels that
he has done the dreadful deed. Question: how closely should we
examine any act of violence that proceeds by means of joint action
on the part of a number of persons?

*And they which heard it, being convicted by their own conscience,
went out one by one, beginning at the eldest . . . (John 8:9).*

Typically, we link "action" with youth. In a group, we tend to
feel that if there is to be response to a dramatic challenge, it will
have to be led by some young person.

Here, however, it is the eldest who leads.

Does first-century cultural emphasis on the dignity of age have
implications for the modern philosophy of retirement, through
which most elders are shelved long before their intellectual and
spiritual peak is reached? How much is our national life affected
by the politician's frank bid for support of the youthful voter?
How may a person of maturity gain respect by virtue of factors
other than his years? Have we made real progress in human affairs
by magnifying the role of youthful leaders? Could a Hitler rise
to power in a society whose young men do not act until given
a sign of leadership by the elders?

*. . . If ye continue in my word, then are ye my disciples indeed
(John 8:31).*

Here is perhaps the most baffling of all tests. Its nature is such
that it cannot be applied with precision, nor can it be defined so
that men of various viewpoints in different epochs will agree upon

its nature. That is to say, this criterion for discipleship is essentially an inner one. Men who differ widely in their basic understanding of Jesus' word, and hence in their practical lives, may be equally convinced that they are continuing in it and are exemplary disciples.

Seen in another light, this is a somewhat camouflaged example of the impossible demand. It leaves the seeker in at least a degree of doubt—which can be constructive, impelling, question-evoking. For, except in a subjective sense, he can never be absolutely sure he is really continuing in the Master's word. So, of all persons, the saint is most likely to be keenly aware that there are respects in which he is not continuing but is falling short. (See verses 37, 43.)

*. . . We be Abraham's seed, and were never in bondage to any man . . . (John 8:33).*

Slavery has no forms so terrible as those which are not recognized. Men can break any chains except those they do not know they wear. Bondage to selfish interest and tawdry values of a culture is more fearful than subjection to a human tyrant.

*. . . I am the light of the world (John 9:5).*

It is this fundamental message, repeated in drama as well as in words, that is proclaimed in events such as the healing of the man blind from birth. Linked with the eye-opening activity of the Saviour, the idea of the "light of the world" gains new depth.

For we ordinarily think of light as merely illuminating. It is true that the divine light does that. But this does not exhaust the work of Jesus. He not only illuminates the external; He also opens the inner eye so that the light from without may penetrate, come to an encounter with a sensitive receptor, and bring revelation.

Considered in this sense, the light-bringing function of Jesus is such that, when made vital in the life of an individual, all perception is transformed. There is no problem that cannot be viewed in the illumination and through the opened eyes of belief. There is no situation that one can even imagine from which divine meaning is absent. In this sense, the Master's light is the philosopher's stone: the key to all knowledge, the elixir of life, the key that opens all locked doors. For when it falls upon the spirit of a man, there is no door that is really shut. Rather, that portal that cannot be forced proves to be simply a pointer that deflects the pilgrim from a path that he, in blindness, would have chosen in preference to a path that will actually prove a short cut on his pilgrimage toward the Eternal City.

*. . . A man that is called Jesus made clay, and anointed mine eyes, and said unto me, Go to the pool of Siloam, and wash: and I went and washed, and I received sight (John 9:11).*

As an explanation for a remarkable healing, this falls far short of what we demand. It simply recounts a series of acts performed in obedience to Jesus, but does not give a logical explanation of why they brought sight to a man born blind. Hence we are not intellectually satisfied any more than were the Pharisees.

Obedience is not identical with or predicated upon understanding. For vital obedience always includes a strong (though not necessarily recognized) element of belief. Men who demand positive profits and final explanations before obeying, make themselves incapable of winning the fruits of obedience. To get the fruits of marriage, one must marry. No amount of imaginative or vicarious seeking can provide a full substitute. One must act in the faith that marriage is good. Refusal to take that plunge effectively closes the door. Just so, there are times when it is imperative to obey Jesus without having the remotest understanding of why He commands what He does.

*And it was the sabbath day when Jesus made the clay, and opened his eyes (John 9:14).*

Why so many Sabbath miracles? What does this emphasis say —merely that Jesus is Lord of all rites and institutions?

Something deeper is involved. Healings that violate codes obeyed by the most moral of men are speaking events that say our most revered practices are not to be regarded as on the level of God. For it is false to assume that man ever fully breaks across the gap between creature and Creator. When that gap is forgotten, man begins to play god in the temple, where he then perpetrates some of his most monstrous deeds: in the name of piety.

*Then came the Jews round about him, and said unto him, How long dost thou make us to doubt? If thou be the Christ, tell us plainly (John 10:24).*

A demand such as this includes its own answer—a negative one. It is like insisting, "Prove that you love me." Belief, or lack of it, is internal to the questioner. There is no way whatever to force proof into the mind of one who will not accept it.

*. . . though ye believe not me, believe the works: that ye may know, and believe, that the Father is in me, and I in him (John 10:38).*

Jesus recognizes that His doubters and opponents are having genuine difficulties. Part of the problem stems from their very piety, their loyalty to the established system and its oral traditions plus written Scriptures.

"You may not be able to accept at present the verbal formulas that I apply to Myself," Jesus is saying here. "Very well. Forget them for the moment. Do not attempt to make a neat doctrinal system just now. Ponder the meaning of My deeds; come to an understanding of their significance for your life. When you have reached this understanding through experience, it will be time enough to try to verbalize this new truth and fit it into your system of thought."

This is very close to the point of view that evoked the cry: "I believe; help thou mine unbelief." The difference is that in the instance John reports here, seekers are limited by the fact that they try to proceed from an outpost camp that is still within the old system. In order to succeed in the quest, they must turn their backs on that system for the moment and seek new meaning in events; when it has been found, it may be coordinated with the old system. To attempt to proceed simply by refining and extending elements from the inherited pattern is futile. It may produce endless arguments and commentaries, but will never yield a fresh gospel.

*. . . This sickness is not unto death, but for the glory of God, that the Son of God might be glorified thereby (John 11:4).*

This is potentially true of any illness!

That illness which is victorious and which glorifies God cannot end in death. Death may, of course, be involved. But death is not here a terminus. It is simply a stage in a journey that leads into a distant and glorious country. Let the sickbed be a place of witness and of victory!

*. . . Lazarus was one of them that sat at the table with him (John 12:2).*

What? A man once dead but now alive is attending a supper?

There are many suggestions here. Even a man brought from the dead, spiritually, doesn't have to be morbid, withdrawn, and pallid; he can still enjoy life's good things. When a man is brought from the dead, his friends and relatives should treat him as a normal person, not a freak to be made Exhibit A in a religious side show.

*. . . they came not for Jesus' sake only, but that they might see Lazarus also, whom he had raised from the dead (John 12:9)*

Inherent in the nature of the stupendous event is the possibility that many (if indeed, not the majority of men) will seize upon it as a mere freak. They will see meaning in it, of course. But the meaning that they find is far from the heart of the matter. It is not so much "misunderstood" as understood in an impoverished and anemic fashion. The curious really do "understand," but see only a marvel that leads to gaping and gossiping; the deeply sensitive see and understand that the man Jesus holds the keys of the door through which men must walk if they are to enter life. He is, in fact, the very door itself.

*These things understood not his disciples at the first: but when Jesus was glorified, then remembered they that these things were written of him, and that they had done these things unto him (John 12:16).*

A single transforming event can shout with such convincing power that the hearer is transformed—converted, in every sense of the word. Such is the dynamic of this process that it may result in re-interpretation of all past events. It literally leads to creation of a whole new complex of memories and understandings.

This power of "conversion," which has capacity to make a new individual every time it occurs, is the most tremendous fact about human life. There are no really closed doors. Every man can be transformed—not just once, but repeatedly. Each fresh transformation rests on those achieved before, so may be higher and more sweeping. From this viewpoint, there is unlimited potential for human growth and transformation.

*For this cause the people also met him, for that they heard that he had done this miracle (John 12:18).*

Jesus never performed spectacular acts either for the sake of the deeds themselves or in order to attract crowds. His miracles always had meaning beyond themselves. Still, the marvelous act served as a stimulus to popular interest.

Such interest is a valid by-product, but to make it an end-product is to pervert one's motives. Religious leaders cannot afford to seek the spectacular for the sake of attracting crowds, but must never shirk from the masses that flock forward as a

118

result of spectacular events which occur as by-products of spiritual searching.

*... Walk while ye have the light, lest darkness come upon you ... (John 12:35).*

Action is imperative. Light, however brilliant, is fleeting. If spiritual light is not used and acted upon at once, the opportunity is forever lost. So in a sense, this is a call to impulsive action of a rather deliberate sort!

Men who ponder whether or not to use half an hour in study or Bible reading are likely to end by using it in sleep or watching TV. Men who ponder giving half a dollar to a beggar may end by buying cigarettes. Men who wait for high noon to start walking, will have lost the desire by the heat of the day.

*By this shall all men know that ye are my disciples, if ye have love one to another (John 13:35).*

This is the supreme test. On the surface, it seems to be absurdly simple and easy to apply. But in practice it is most difficult. How does one really know whether others have love; what measuring stick shall be used?

We are greatly tempted to settle for easier and more practical standards than that which Jesus proposed. We'd like to decide that discipleship can be defined in such terms as: formal church membership (in a particular communion), participation in a pattern of worship that is accepted in the culture, abstinence from a habit that is branded as evil, liberality in contributions. We don't really want to accept a standard as abstract and challenging as that of love.

*... how can we know the way? (John 14:5).*

Thomas' question echoes a perennial one of the human heart. It stems from Jesus' discussion of the way that leads to God's mansions and His eternal reward. Though eager to reach that goal, one may be sincerely puzzled as to the way he should follow in searching for it.

In a sense that is much deeper than a mere figure of speech, Jesus Himself is the Way. He is the living path that men must tread in order to reach goal's end. That is, the way is not like a path traced on a map—fixed, immovable, and static. Rather, the way is living personality; the way is vital, capable of entering into dynamic relationships with the pilgrims who walk it—and therefore far from "identical" in any frozen sense in the various situations of encounter. Two pilgrims, each walking the way, are not necessarily in identical situations and do not necessarily follow precisely the same path in every respect.

This is at once the marvel and the mystery and the stumbling block of Christianity. Many sincere seekers balk at the simple grandeur of it, and try to reduce the gospel from living encounter with a Person to a fixed and static legal system.

*If ye abide in me, and my words abide in you, ye shall ask what ye will, and it shall be done unto you (John 15:7).*

Here is a key to many vexatious problems of prayer. One in whom Jesus' words abide is literally and dramatically transformed, made new—and redirected. If Jesus' words have truly lodged in the spirit in that deep sense, one's wants and goals are reshaped in such fashion that he is incapable of praying for things out of harmony with the Master's message. He will pray only for the good things that the Father is already yearning to bestow and has ready in outstretched hands to confer on those who want these things sufficiently to accept them. Most of the problems of "unanswered prayer" come to focus here. (See verse 16, and John 16:24.)

*These things have I spoken unto you, that ye should not be offended (John 16:1).*

Possibilities for offense, in this sense, are enormous and varied.

It is easy to become offended with our critics, and our opponents, and our persecutors. For Jesus has just warned that Christianity involves a minority position.

Perhaps this is an aspect of the valley of the shadow of death, through which none can pass unscathed—*i.e.*, without taking offense—except as he is shielded by God.

Again, it is possible to be offended in a more inclusive sense. Weary and discouraged by the troubles that are linked with and which may actually stem from a minority position, one may end by chucking the whole business. He may give up active Christian discipleship, get out of the church in disgust, surrender to demonic forces that plague every man who tries to walk the always difficult way of life. With consciousness of the fact that temptation to be offended comes to everyone, it is perhaps a trifle easier to be faithful and joyous under trial. Lacking awareness that trials are inevitable, a beginning pilgrim may be tempted to give up after a few hard bumps.

*. . . your heart shall rejoice, and your joy no man taketh from you (John 16:22).*

Only nonmaterial things are really safe! Only ideas and values and loyalties are of such nature that no man can seize them even at gun point. Brain-washing is perhaps the nearest approach to taking basic joy from a man. But the wreck that has been successfully brain-washed is no longer a full man; the spirit has fled. In the process of "taking," the self has been destroyed.

Men may take from other men everything—even life—with the exception of joys, beliefs, hopes, convictions, ideals, and dedications.

*These things have I spoken unto you, that in me ye might have peace . . . (John 16:33).*

This is simply a vivid instance of a note that runs through much of Scripture—from Psalm 23 to all the Gospels and most of Paul's letters. Jesus' peace is not "the power of positive thinking." Rather, it is a strange and not wholly logical or definable peace-in-tribulation.

This paradoxical situation grows out of the inherent dualism of man. Man is a creature who is trapped in space and time—but he is also a soul that has neither temporal nor physical limits. This double-sided being lives in a space-time world in which his soul is never fully contained. His stay in this material world is briefer than that of an insect in the larval home; all his enduring values center in a "world beyond" which is not within time or space.

Hence it is not simply possible, but altogether likely, that the person who lives in radiant inner victory may be deeply involved in outward circumstances which seem to other persons merely unadulterated tribulation. Material success and failure have nothing to do with Jesus' peace; the man who is peaceful-in-turmoil may be a great success in his mundane undertakings—or he may be a colossal failure.

*And this is life eternal, that they might know thee the only true God, and Jesus Christ, whom thou hast sent (John 17:3).*

Life eternal is not a temporal state or a physical condition; it is beyond these categories and transcends definition. It cannot be demonstrated in logic, but may be known in experience. It is that mystical state of being that grows out of continuing encounter between man and God. It is as much a fruit of attitude as of event. Any attempt to bring this state into greater concreteness results in distortion. Even the most sublime metaphors of the Revelation simply hint at and point toward ideas they do not fully contain. Eternal life is a relationship with God, through Christ. We know that it is therefore good. No other data are needed.

*. . . a garden . . . (John 18:1).*

This is the place of betrayal. In the moment of agony, it contrasts strongly with those ideas which produced the hymn, "I Come to the Garden Alone."

A garden, street corner, drug store, courthouse, office, kitchen, schoolroom, or any other place whatever gains its significance from actions of those individuals for whom it is a stage. From pool room to prayer cell, there is no automatic, inherent character in a place. A garden can be a trysting spot for Christ and His beloved—or it can be a place of perfidy.

It is the individual, the man, who gives both meaning and direction to the places in which he plays his role in life's drama.

*. . . they themselves went not into the judgment hall, lest they should be defiled; but that they might eat the passover (John 18:28).*

This is perhaps the most dramatic instance in world literature in which men seek ritual purity while precipitating an act of violence.

Never assume that these killers were consciously evil. Far from it. They acted in good conscience—even holy integrity, as they conceived it.

Let us guard against taking part in any group movement that will lead to crucifying a man for the sake of established rites and customs.

*Pilate saith unto him, What is truth? . . . (John 18:38).*

Though cast in the form of a question, this does not constitute an inquiry. It is the voice of the scoffer—the man who is sure that there is no truth. It is not a request for guidance, but a repudiation of the possibility that a guide exists. It comes from the depths of skepticism. It is the voice of one who cannot be led, because he believes in the meaninglessness of things. His belief inhibits discovery. For him, there actually is no "truth" in the deepest sense, for he is incapable of coming into encounter with it in its character of truth.

*. . . We have a law, and by our law he ought to die . . . (John 19:7).*

At their highest, laws are man-made and limited. At their lowest, they are ludicrous or fiendish. Let us be careful not to sink to the level of legalism in our evaluation of our associates.

*. . . If thou let this man go, thou art not Caesar's friend (John 19:12).*

This is a powerful argument. It is often employed in situations where leaders face difficult decisions. In such a case, there is no way to keep everyone satisfied. One must inevitably displease one faction or another; the choice is simply which to offend.

Religious leaders face this dilemma frequently. They, too, are challenged not to break friendship with Caesar. Yet it is a major problem to identify the Caesars of an epoch; in some instances, they are members of one's congregation.

*. . . it was written in Hebrew, and Greek, and Latin (John 19:20).*

The precise pattern of events leading to the crucifixion could have taken place only in a polyglot culture. Hebrew law and tradition were no more essential than Greek philosophy plus Roman government.

In God's providence, every cultural context presents special characteristics and unique opportunities. We have no need to bemoan problems of our day. Rather, we need to seek to discover God's special acts and revelations that could not intelligibly occur in any other cultural context.

From this viewpoint, every "today" is special, exciting, and adventurous. It is a medium through which God is shouting—if we will listen and understand. To focus zealous attention upon the first-century culture that formed a background for Jesus' ministry, to attempt to duplicate some selected fragment of "New Testament society," is to distort the possibilities of revelation in our own day. Because God made and sustained it, this day is just as holy and sacred as the first century—if we will but treat it so.

*They said therefore among themselves, Let us not rend it . . .*
*(John 19:24).*

To the Roman soldiers who made up the execution squad, the taking of Jesus' life was a casual matter. But the question of cutting or tearing a seamless robe was a matter of some importance. To put knife to cloth seemed a desecration of something fine and rather rare—while it was a matter of trivial significance to thrust a spear into the side of a man.

More concerned over a garment than a life!

Cruel and violent though this seems, it marks our day fully as much as the first century. In the machine age, it is not uncommon for a manufactured product to be elevated to much higher status than some men enjoy in society, for instance, the operators of some machines, vagrants, "consumers," the handicapped, "the public."

*. . . supposing him to be the gardener . . . (John 20:15).*

Such is God's vital Word that it is most difficult to distinguish between the Word made flesh and any ordinary gardener. Possibilities of human-divine dialogue are unlimited. God can speak through any event, any person, any circumstance, any word. But for those whose eyes are dim and whose ears are dull, even the most dramatic of all God's words—the Word incarnate—may be misunderstood, pushed casually aside, regarded as commonplace and meaningless.

*Then Jesus saith unto them, Children, have ye any meat? . . .*
*(John 21:5).*

Use of the title "Children" cannot have been accidental.

Jesus' use of it in addressing the disciples in His resurrection

125

seems to be a way of saying to these men that they are still far from expert. They still have much to learn. And, like children, they still have capacity to learn.

One who takes great pride in achievement is likely to resent being addressed by such a title. Only those who know their lack of achievement will accept it calmly. To the degree that one reacts emotionally when dubbed a boy still under instruction, he shows that he lacks the very qualities of childhood that Jesus so often stresses.

A child, in spite of flashing periods of overconfidence, usually knows that he doesn't know. Hence he is eager to learn. He so earnestly wants to learn to read that he pressures his parents to buy an extra copy of the first-grade reader to keep at home; then he joyfully reads aloud, simultaneously proving and increasing his skill.

When one forgets, even briefly, that he does not really know, he begins to preen himself with having arrived. He may glory in a title such as "expert" or "specialist"—and in doing so, inhibits all possibility of continuous learning, growth, creativity, insight.

Even after a firsthand encounter with the risen Saviour, every disciple needs constantly to remind himself that he is a beginner with much to learn.